Guns That Talk

Firearms with Unique Histories

Vol. I

Compiled, Edited and Published by
L&R Books, Livonia, New York U.S.A.

Copyright 1999 by LaFever and Root Books

Lafever and Root Books

4447 East Lake Road, Livonia, New York USA

Phone 716-346-2577

Fax 716-346-4512

Email Bookman1@AOL.COM
or Bigmick45@WEBTV.NET

ISBN 1-884849-31-8

About the publishers Mick (on the left) and Larry (on the right)

Malcolm "Mick" LaFever lives in Avon, NY. He and his wife, Rhonda have one son Josiah. Upon graduation from high school, Mick enlisted in the United States Army. After two tours as a Military Police Officer, he left the service, a highly decorated soldier and police veteran and joined civilian law enforcement. Presently he is working as a Private Investigator. Mick is a member of the NRA and The American Legion. His interest in firearms and western memorabilia began in the early 1970s. As well as collecting for his own pleasure, he buys, sells and authenticates guns and other items from the periods of the Civil War, Indian Wars and the Frontier West.

Larry Root lives in Livonia, NY with his wife Karen, two dogs, two cats, one horse and numerous lizards. Larry's two children Larry jr. and Betsy are busy building their adult lives in Miami, FL and Bronxville, NY respectively. Larry is a graduate of the University of Rochester, The Rochester Institute of Technology, an Air Force veteran and a Life member of the NRA. He has had a life long interest in gun collecting, firearms and target shooting. In his travels in the western United States, he discovered and became interested in historical firearms and associated curios and relics. In response to the interest and support of fellow collectors, as well as a decade's experience in the gun book publishing business, he and Mick decided it would be an important contribution to compile an illustrated book of "Guns That Talk". By drawing on some of the country's premier collections as well as their own, this book has been assembled.

We both hope you enjoy this trip back in time and enjoy each firearm's unique history.

Acknowledgments

This book could not have been produced without the assistance of many people.

Our fellow gun collectors have been unfailing kind and considerate in sharing their treasures with us.

In addition our good friend, John Hart, "The Lone Ranger" assisted us in many ways. And, as in all our endeavors, the constant help and support of our families has been indispensable.

The following is only a partial list of those who have made this book possible;

Dr. Henry Alperin	James Pilchak
Steve Elliot	Ben Powell
R.D. Fendley	Ike Robertson
Richard Harris	Charles Schreiner
Gary Helin	Paul Sorrell
Jerry Hemphill	John Stewart
Mike Holloway	Kit Stewart
Ralph L. Hooker	David Tate
Kurt House	G.R. Taylor
Lee Hutcheson	Texas Ranger Hall of Fame
Elbridge LaFever	Ramona Turmon
Bob Land	Ken Unger
Charles McGraw	Lew Wight

BUFFALO ON MILLER BROS 101 RANCH

Dedication

We wish to dedicate this book to our families, who have been most helpful and tolerant of the hours we have spent away from them while researching, photographing, meeting with fellow collectors and huddled around the faithful Macintosh. Also a special dedication to Thomas Lijewski, Phil Osterling and Roger Linton, three good friends and fellow enthusiasts who have gone on before us to that big collectors' show "way up yonder".

Introduction

On the pages of this book you will see and learn about various firearms. each with its own unique history.

If you are like us, history and arms enthusiasts, you will enjoy sitting back in your favorite chair and turning each page that takes you back, gazing into nostalgic yesteryear.

Whether it's "Hi-Yo Silver Away", or "Reach for the Sky" all these guns have fascinating
stories to tell.

All part of our great American Heritage!

One can only wonder what they would have to say, if only these guns could talk.............

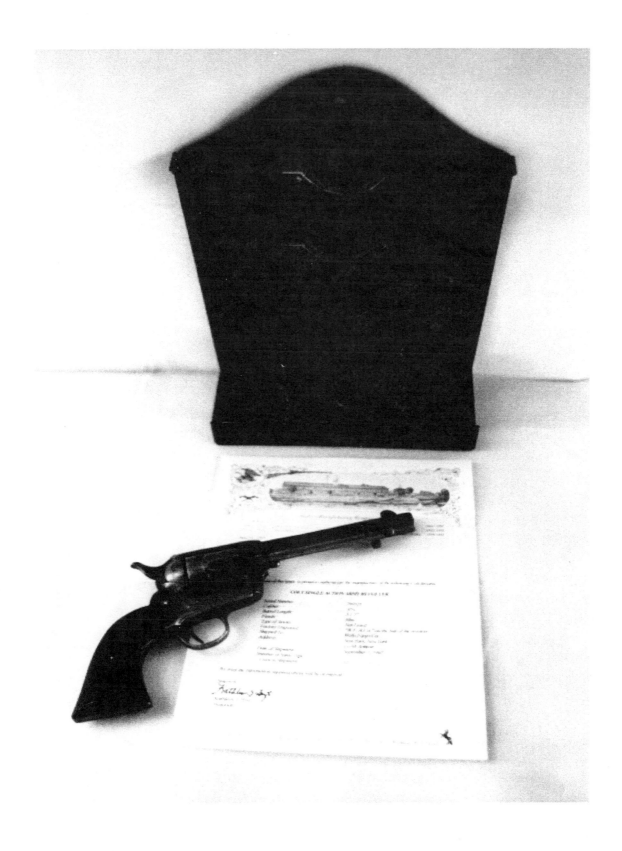

A Colt SAA, 45 LC 5&1/2" bbl., serial #299525, factory engraved on the butt "WF & CO". It is shown with a rare early Wells Fargo & Co. letter box and the Colt Firearms factory letter confirming the description and the sale of the revolver to Wells Fargo & Co..

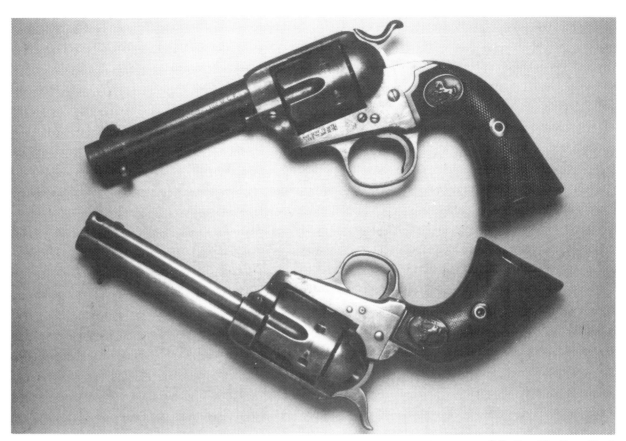

Collection of Dr. Henry Alperin

SN 228465. Bisley Model (top) SN 228437 Single Action Army (Bottom). These Colts are from the same shipment from Colt on June 18, 1902 to Turner Hardware Co., Muskogee, Oklahoma (Indian Territory). Both are .32-20 cal., 4 3/4" barrel length, and are blue in finish.

Collection of Dr. Henry Alperin

SN 228465 Bisley Model (top) SN 228437 Single Action Army (bottom). View of underside showing frame and triggerguard numbers. Colt records indicate that these revolvers were in same shipment to Muskogee, Oklahoma (Indian Territory).

Collection of Dr. Henry Alperin

SN 166072. This early Bisley Model .44-40 cal. 7 1/2" bbl. was shipped from Colt Firearms on January 18, 1898 to Colt's Patent Firearms Co., San Francisco Agency, San Francisco, California. (Note Colt Frontier Six Shooter on barrel)

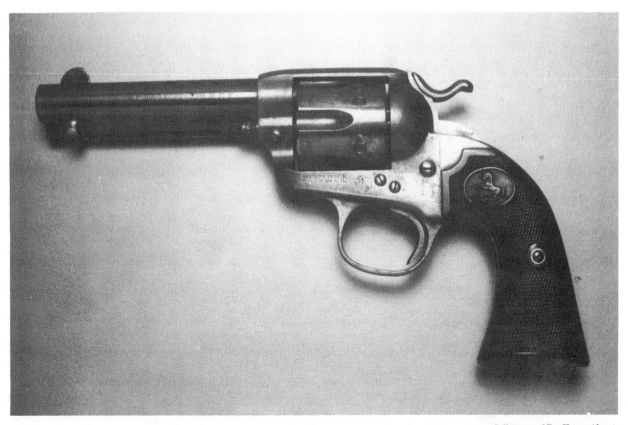

Collection of Dr. Henry Alperin

SN 196688. This Bisley Model .38-40 cal., 4 3/4" barrel, blue finish, was shipped from the Colt Factory on June 25, 1900 to J. F. Schmelzer & Sons Arms Co., Kansas City, Kansas.

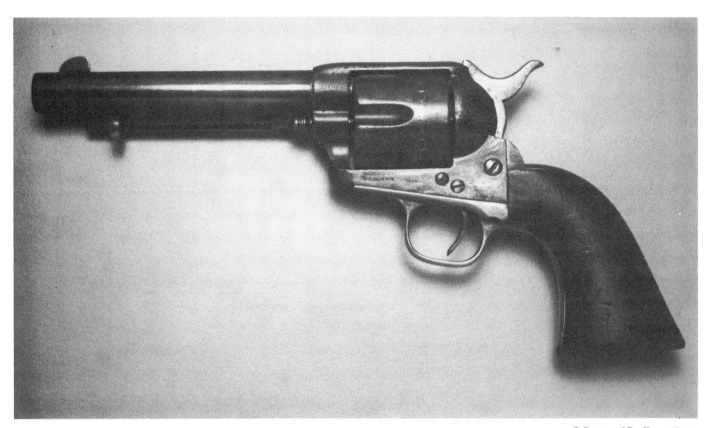

SN 450. This early production frame military artillery was originally issued to the 6th or 10th Cavalry units from Ft. Leavenworth, Kansas Arsenal in 1873.

SN 450. View showing early 450 frame number and triggerguard #192. This Artillery probably saw action in the Indian Wars.

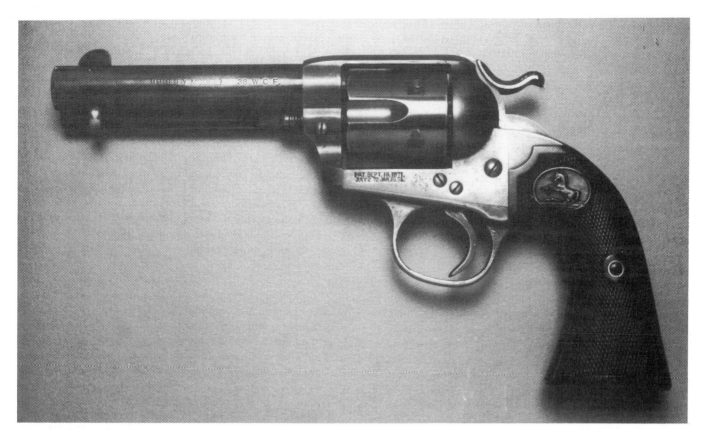

Collection of Dr. Henry Alperin

SN 277582. This Bisley Model .38-40 .al. 4 3/4" barrel, blue finish revolver was shipped from the Colt factory on June 6, 1906 to A. Steinfeld & Co., Tucson, Arizona.

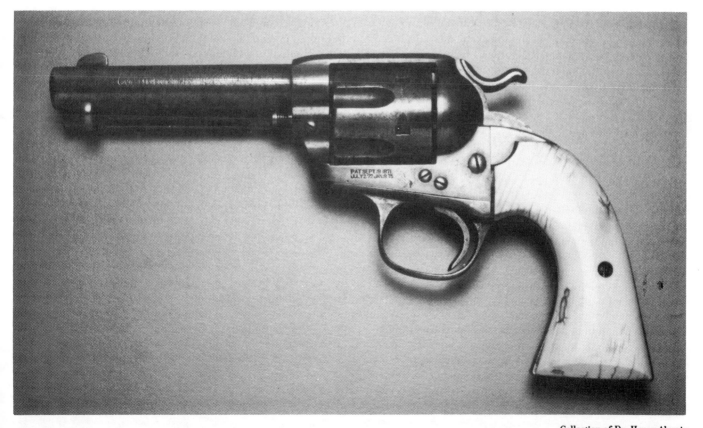

Collection of Dr. Henry Alperin

SN 292227. Colt records indicate this Bisley Model .44-40 cal., 4 3/4" barrel, blue finish revolver was shipped on April 12, 1907 to Quintana Hermanoz, City of Mexico, Mexico City, Mexico. Note the old Ivory grips.

Collection of Dr. Henry Alperin

SN 306926. Colt factory records show this Bisley Model .32-20 cal. 4 3/4" barrel, blue finish revolver was shipped on December 12, 1908, to Richards and Conover Hardware Co., Kansas City, Missouri.

END OF ALPERIN COLLECTION

Private Collection

SN 320616. This .41 cal., 4 3/4" bbl., blue finish revolver was manufactured in 1911 and was the personal sidearm of Texas Ranger Harrison Hamer. He was a brother to Texas Ranger Frank Hamer of Bonnie & Clyde fame. No factory information is available.

Len R. McFarlane
Deputy U. S. Marshal
Southern District, State of Texas

Len R. McFarlane was a native of Richmond, Texas, one of eight children of Isaac and Sally McFarlane. He was born in 1868 and died in 1925. He served as U. S. Deputy Marshal for Harris County, Texas, from 1910 until 1924. He was first listed in the 1910 Houston City directory "Deputy United States Marshal, office, 305 Paul Building, residence, Baltimore Hotel, 910 1/2 Fannin." He remained a bachelor throughout his lifetime and became the protective benefactor of his namesake niece, Len McFarlane who lost her parents at an early age. While serving as U. S. Deputy Marshal, he acquired a Colt single action revolver, fully engraved, with carved pearl grips serial number 314770.

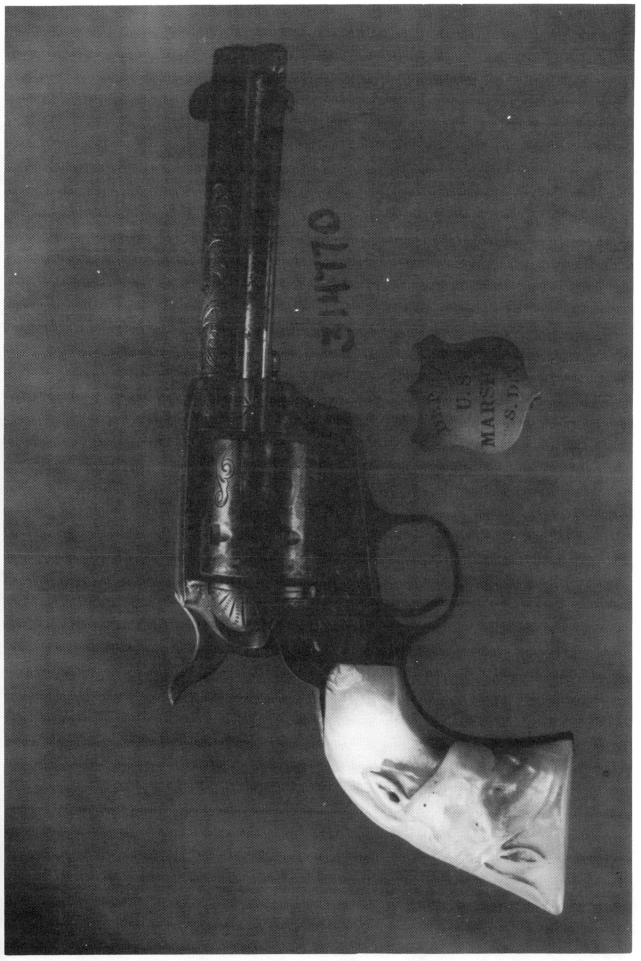

SA 314770. Colt Records indicate this .45 cal., 4 3/4" bbl., nickel finish revolver was factory engraved and shipped October 10, 1910, to H & D Folsom Arms Co., New York, New York. Shipment of two. This revolver was the sidearm of Len R. McFarlane, U. S. Deputy Marshal for Harris County, Texas from 1910 until 1924. The carved pearl stocks were probably fitted by the New York dealer.

Collection of Dick Burdick

Collection of Robert S. Clegg

SN 118937. This .45 cal., 4 3/4 bbl. manufactured in 1886 was used by Oklahoma Sheriff Jess Phillips. It also saw service on the "KATY" railroad.

Jess Phillips
"KATY" RR Engineer & Oklahoma Sheriff

This gun was associated with the famous Missouri, Kansas, & Texas railroad that operated through Indian Territory (Oklahoma). The railroad was called the "KATY" RR. Jess Phillips was an engineer on the KATY and used the gun at that time and later used it when elected sheriff of Coal County, Oklahoma. He was the second sheriff of Coal County and carried it for the eight years he served. The gun was later carried by Thea H. Bonner, a friend of Jess Phillips and peace officer in Oklahoma for 26 years.

The KATY was a famous western R.R. that ran through such famous towns as Houston, Fort Worth, Waco, Wichita Falls, Denison, McAlster, Muskogee, Tulsa, Kansas City, Topeka, and St. Louis. The R.R. was plagued with train robberies throughout the Indian Territory and the old Colt was a welcome companion to the engineer.

A very interesting "Colt" with association with two western lawmen (Oklahoma) and the famous KATY railroad during the Indian period and R.R. holdup era.

An original "KATY" stock certificate.

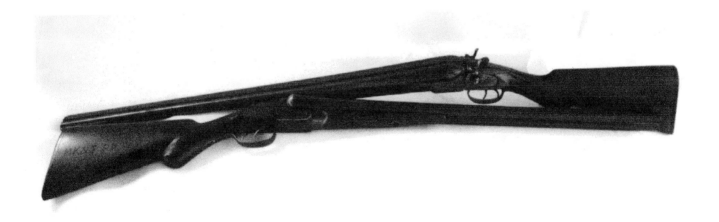

Two shotguns used on the Missouri, Kansas and Texas Railway. The upper is an American Gun Co. 12 gauge serial #306225 with 30" bbls.. The lower is also another American Gun Co. 12 gauge serial #7103 with 26" bbls. Both guns have fluid steel barrels and are marked "MK&T RR" on the buttstocks.

Collection of R. D. Fendley

SN 122358. This rare "Sheriff's Model" .45 cal., with 3 1/2" bbl. left the Colt Factory on January 15, 1893, and was shipped to the Dunlay and Geisler Company, Houston, Texas. Shipment of three. Shown with original sheriff's model holster.

Collection of R. D. Fendley

SN 163951. This .32-20 cal., 4 3/4" bbl. was factory engraved and shipped from Colt on April 10, 1896, to Hibbard, Spencer, Bartlett & Co., Chicago, Illinois, c/o N.Y. Newby Trustee. Shipment of two. This rare engraved .32-20 now has ivory stocks, but was shipped with rubber. Shown with assortment of early leather holsters.

Collection of R. D. Fendley

SN 64425. This fine .44-40 cal. 7 1/2" bbl. revolver was manufactured in 1881. No record is available but the nickel finish and the one-piece walnut grips are original. Note the "Colt Frontier Six Shooter" legend on barrel. Shown here with old money belt and double-loop holster.

Collection of R. D. Fendley

SN 115860. This .44-40, 4 3/4" bbl. nickel finish revolver letters "all the way." Records indicate this gun left the Colt Factory with ivory grips on October 29, 1885, bound for the Commings & Geisler Company in Houston, Texas. Shipment of one.

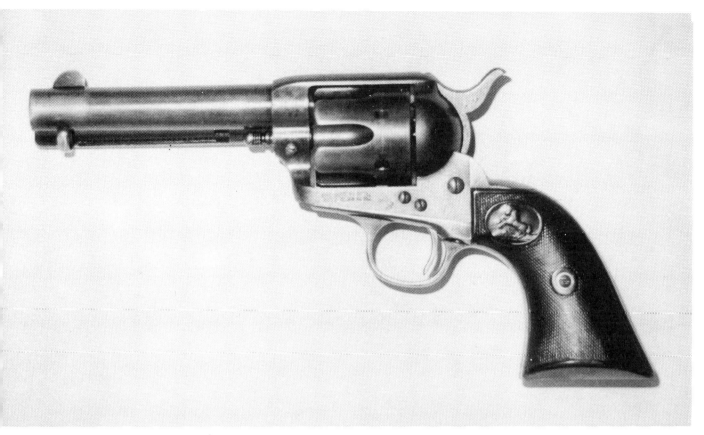

Collection of R. D. Fendley

N 203978. This .45 cal., 4 3/4" bbl., blue finish revolver was shipped January 4, 1901, to the Copper Queen Consolidated Mining, c/o Detroit Copper Mining Co., Morenci, Arizona. Twenty-four in shipment.

The Copper Queen

Much glamour and legend surround the history of the Copper Queen Consolidated Mining Co. It was discovered in 1877 and after much expansion developed into a magnificent copper enterprise. In 1855 two mines, the Atlantic and Copper Queen were joined in the name of Copper Queen Consolidated Mining Company and owned by the Phelps Dodge Corporation. In 1917 the name Copper Queen Consolidated Mining Company was changed to Phelps Dodge & Company.

The Copper Queen was to be the first of many mines in the Southwest to become one of the nations leading producers of copper. The Copper Queen purchased many Colt Single Action revolvers. The only way to authenticate a Copper Queen Colt is by a factory letter from Colt Firearms indicating the number of guns in shipment and the date.

(1) Early 1900s Cap Box (2) Miner's Shovel (3) Colt SA Serial # 330016 .45 cal., 4 3/4" bbl. Shipped July 9, 1913, to Phelps-Dodge Mercantile, Douglas, Arizona. Two in shipment. The factory records state that these two revolvers were fitted with long flute cylinders. (4) Early Copper Queen Guard badge (5) Colt SA Serial # 250175, .45 cal., 4 3/4" bbl. Shipped Feb. 4, 1904 to Copper Queen Consolidated Mining Co., Bisbee, Arizona. Five in shipment. (6) Colt SA Bisley model Serial # 287474, .45 cal., 5 1/2" bbl. Shipped Feb. 8, 1907, to Copper Queen Consolidated Mining Co. in Douglas, Arizona. Five in shipment. (7) Colt SA Serial # 220040, .44-40 cal., 4 3/4" bbl. Shipped Jan. 4, 1902 to Copper Queen Consolidated Mining Co. Twenty-five in shipment. (8) Colt SA Serial # 276676, 38-40 Cal., 4 3/4" bbl. Shipped March 30, 1906 to Copper Queen Mining Company, Bisbee, Arizona. Three in shipment. (9) Colt SA Serial # 203978, .45 cal., 4 3/4" bbl. Shipped on Jan. 4, 1901, to Copper Queen Consolidated Mining Company, c/o Detroit Copper Mining Co. in Morenci, Arizona. Twenty-four in Shipment. (10) Colt SA Serial # 154357, .44-40 cal., 4 3/4" bbl. with Eagle grips. Shipped on Dec. 4, 1895 to the Arizona Copper Co. (no address). Twelve in shipment. (11) Colt SA Bisley Model Serial # 253802, .32-20 cal., 4 3/4" bbl. Shipped April 9, 1904, to Copper Queen Consolidated Mining Co., Bisbee, Arizona. Four in shipment. (12) Colt SA Serial # 316384, .32-20 cal., 4 3/4" bbl. Shipped March 10, 1911 to Phelps Dodge & Co., c/o Detroit Copper Corp., Bisbee, Arizona. Three in shipment. (13) Colt SA Serial # 198557 rare .38 Colt cal., 4 3/4" bbl. Shipped Aug. 10, 1900 to Copper Queen Consolidated Mining Co., Bisbee Arizona. Four in shipment (14) Early 1900s Dynamite box. All the items & guns above are shown on and around an early pack saddle.

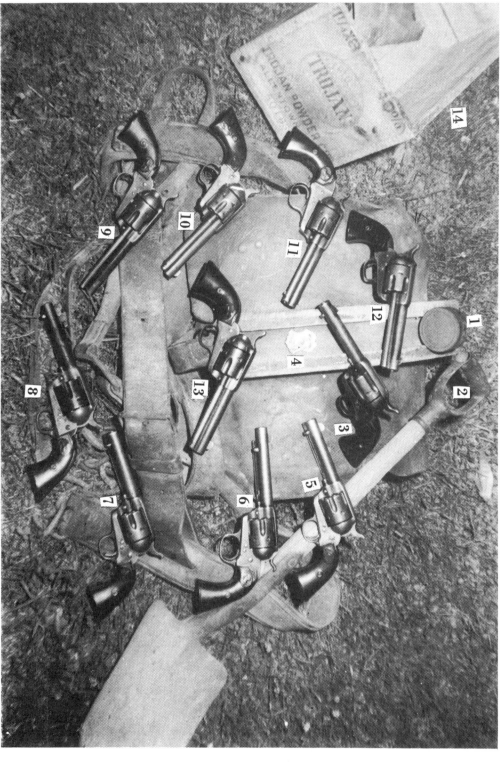

Collection of R. D. Fendley

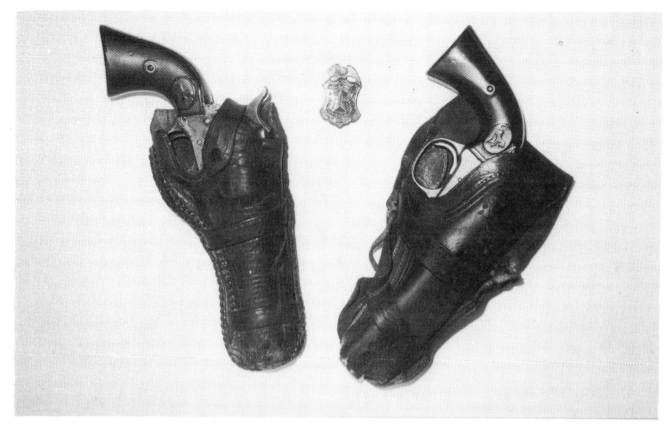

Collection of R. D. Fendley

An interesting photo showing two Copper Queen revolvers in their original holsters. Left is Serial # 220040, .44-40 cal. and right is Serial # 253802 Bisley model. Center is an early Copper Queen badge.

Collection of R. D. Fendley

SN 330016. This rare long fluted model .45 cal., 4 3/4" bbl. was shipped on July 9, 1913, to Phelps-Dodge Mercantile, Douglas, Arizona. Two in shipment.

SN 253802. Bisley Model .32-20, 4 3/4" bbl. blue finish. Shipped April 9, 1904, to Copper Queen Consolidated Mining Co., Bisbee, Arizona.

Top Left: SN 316384, .32-20 cal. Shipped on Mar. 10, 1911, to Phelps Dodge & Co. c/o Detroit Copper Corp. Second Left: SN 154357, .44-40 cal. Shipped Dec. 4, 1893, to Arizona Copper Co. Top Right: SN 330016, .45 cal. Shipped on July 9, 1913 to Phelps-Dodge Mercantile, Douglas, Arizona. Bottom Middle: SN 198557, .38 Colt cal. Shipped on Aug. 10, 1900 to Copper Queen Consolidated Mining Co. Bisbee, Arizona. Bottom Right: 220040, .44-40 cal. Shipped on Jan. 4, 1902, to Copper Queen Consolidated Mining Co., Bisbee, Arizona.

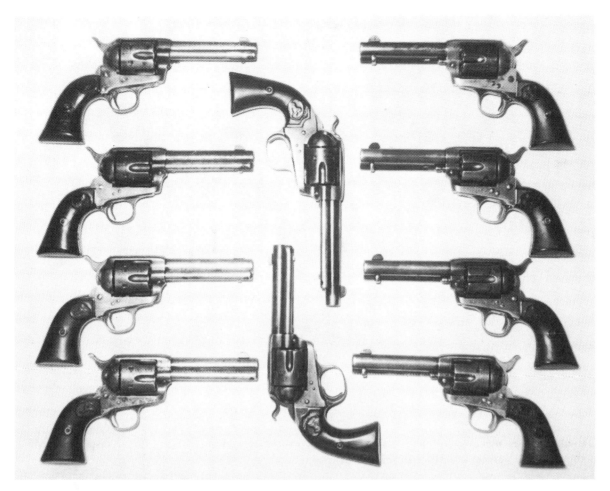

Interesting photo showing various calibers & two Bisleys. All were shipped to Arizona mining companies.

Top: SN 289474 Bisley Model, .45 cal. Shipped Feb. 8, 1907, to Copper Queen Consolidated Mining Co., Douglas, Arizona. Bottom: SN 253802 Bisley Model .32-20 cal. Shipped April 9, 1904, to Copper Queen Consolidated Mining Co., Bisbee, Arizona.

Collection of R. D. Fendley

SN 19154. This rare nickel plated U.S. Calvary .45 cal. manufactured in 1881 is a Casey inspected revolver and is shown with a correct 1881 flap U.S. holster.

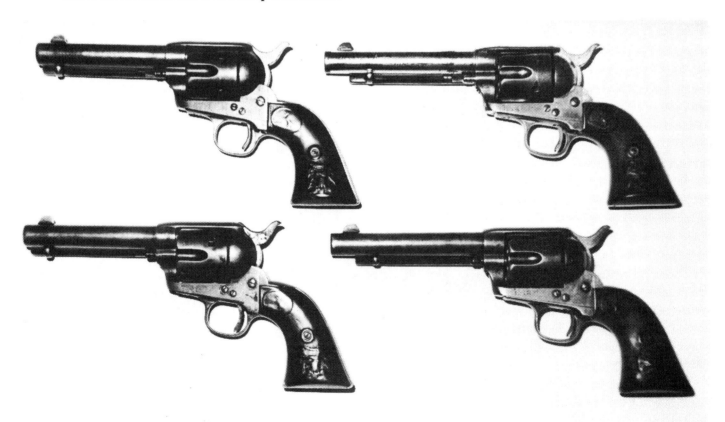

Collection of R. D. Fendley

SN 125763 & 125764. (left) These .44-40 cal., etched panel, 4 3/4" barrel Colt Frontier Six-Shooters are consecutively numbered. They were manufactured in 1888 and no Factory information is available. (right) SN 106949 (top) and SN 100218. These are the scarce 5 1/2" barrel, etched panel, .44-40 Colt Frontier Six-Shooters. All these revolvers are in very good condition.

END OF FENDLEY COLLECTION

Collection of Jim Gossett

SN 278790. Colt records this interesting information on this .44-40 cal., 4 3/4" bbl., blue finish revolver. It was shipped June 13, 1906, to McIntosh Hardware Co., Albuquerque, Territory of New Mexico, c/o Winchester Repeating Arms Co. Shipment of ten. It later saw use as a movie gun with Fox Studios.

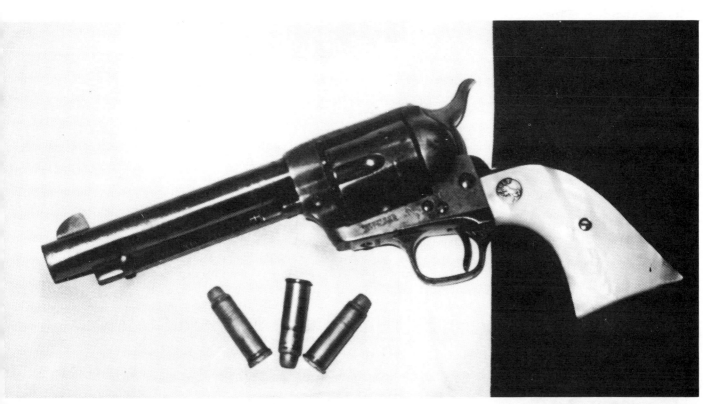

Collection of Jim Gossett

SN 336787. This .45 cal., 5 1/2" bbl., blue finish revolver was shipped in 1917 to El Paso, Texas. Under the right grip is "T. Brass, Capt. Signal Corps, Feb.5, 1918". Under the left grip is "Camp Lewis WN. 123rd Field Sig. Batt."

Collection of Jink and Wanda Howard

This Colt SA .45 cal., 5 1/2" bbl., blue finish revolver was shipped March 17, 1958, directly to Audie Murphy, North Hollywood, California. Shipment of two. Most of the original finish is remaining.

Audie Murphy's Colt SAA

Audie Murphy

Audie Murphy was born June 20, 1924 in Hunt County, Texas, a few miles from Farmersville. He enlisted in the Army in 1942 at the age of eighteen. He served in the European Theater during WW II. He received more medals than any other soldier in American History, one being the Congressional Medal of Honor.

After coming home he went to Hollywood, California where he made thirty-nine movies in which he played the leading roll and five movies in which he had supporting roles. Most of these movies were western, but probably his greatest was the movie "To Hell and Back." This movie was about his experiences while in the Army. He died in a plane crash in 1971.

At the height of his movie career Colt sent him two .45 SA Colts. Since Audie was a simple man he wanted simple guns.

This is an unusual photo of Cowboy and Western star Randolph Scott because he is not carrying the trademark Colt SAA that every good and bad guy had slung from their hips.
In this autographed, but as yet unidentified, movie publicity still, Scott has a Colt New Service in his holster. The revolver itself, caliber 45 Long Colt, is pictured below and is engraved "Randolph Scott" on the backstrap. Perhaps it was a favorite of his and therefore he chose to feature it in this photograph. Another mystery from a gun that is keeping its secrets.

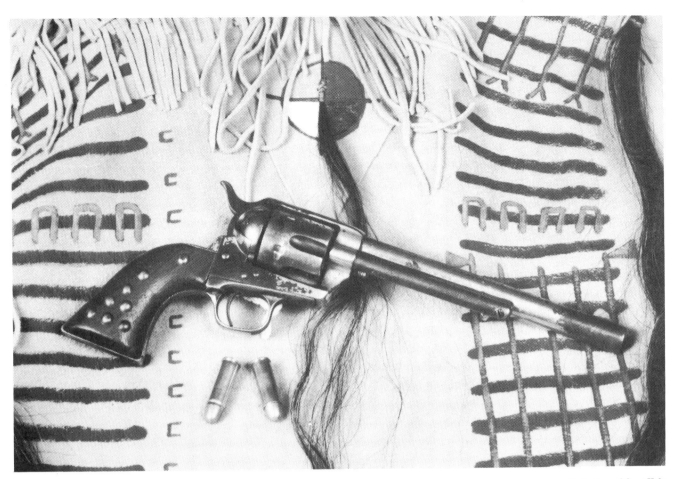

Collection of Gary Helin

Serial No. 60838. Tacked Indian Colt 1880 production, David F. Clark, ordinance inspected Colt has very rare nickel finish, all proof marks Visible, but no U.S. stamping. Tacked walnut grips are original, gun was found with matching tacked holster and wide beaded gun belt. Colt factory letter states it was a Government issued revolver.

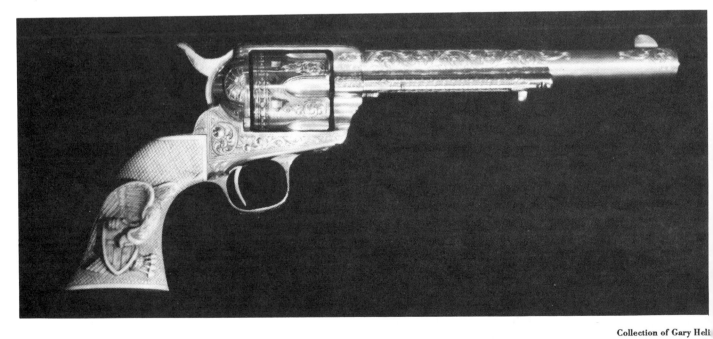

Collection of Gary Helin

Serial No. 15730. This early 1875 production Colt 7 1/2" barreled .45 is decorated in the fullest style of engraving for the period. It retains 85% of its original gold plate. The grips are of checked ivory, right side grip is carved high relief American Eagle and snake, very similar to the grips on the 1861 Colts presented to General Custer. Unfortunately no historical information has been uncovered on this unusual Colt to this date.

Serial No. 135084. Colt letter states 5 1/2" barreled .45, factory engraved, nickel finish. Shipped to Charles Hummel and Sons, September 18, 1890, San Antonio, Texas.

Serial No. 45037. 7 1/2" Colt .45: Blue finish, carved left hand Mexican Eagle ivory grips. Shipped to Simmon's Hardware, St. Louis, Missouri, August of 1880. Unusual features are buckhorn type target rear sight and buntline type front sight. Gun was once the property of Lupe Scranto a known bodyguard of Pancho Villa during the revolution.

Serial No. 13780. Model 3 Smith and Wesson, engraved and inscribed Doroteo Arango. Very possibly the first gun owned by Pancho Villa, as he used his God-given name only until about 17 years of age, known thereafter as Pancho Villa.

Pancho Villa

View of Backstrap

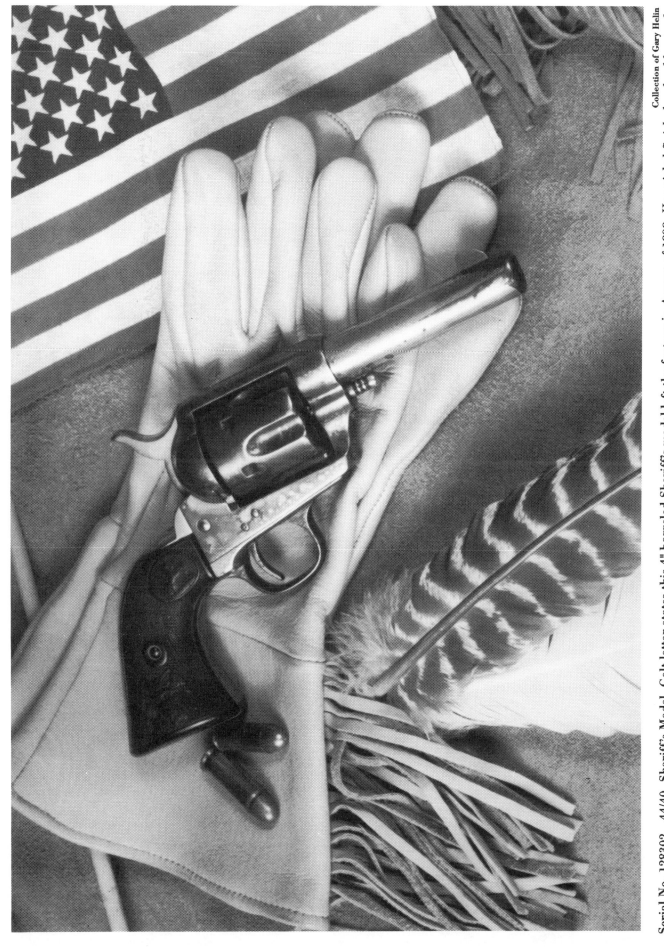

Serial No. 128302. .44/40, Sheriff's Model. Colt letter states this 4" barreled Sheriff's model left the factory in August of 1898. Has nickel finish, hard rubber eagle grips, .44/40 caliber, one-gun special order shipment to H. and D. Folsom Arms, c/o H. L. Dyer. Bottom portion of left grip is stamped W. F. Cody.

Collection of Gary Helin

Early 1860's. Swivel Holster: This rig was handmade to fit only a 1860 army revolver. Lined in brass, and vented to protect the holster when fired without drawing the weapon.

Serial No. 288896. Ranger William E. Cooper's Colt. Beautifully engraved by the famous Texas Engraver, Cole Agee. This blue and case-hardened Colt .38-40 is inscribed "Ranger Wm. E. Cooper presented by M.O.P. Railway Lines." Moody Texas Ranger Library records show Cooper served two enlistments as a special agent from 1933 through 1937.

Collection of Gary Helin

Colt Serial # 149266. .44/40 Gun Belt and Holster, Dodge City: Marked "Wright Beverly and Co., Dodge City, Kansas." Wright and Beverly opened their hardware store in Dodge City in 1877. A fire destroyed the business along with several others including the famous Long Branch Saloon in 1885. The store was never reopened. This early cowboy rig had to have been purchased between 1877 and 1885. The holster, gunbelt, and pearl handled .44/40 was found ninety miles from Dodge City in 1988, over one hundred years after its original owner purchased it in Dodge.

29

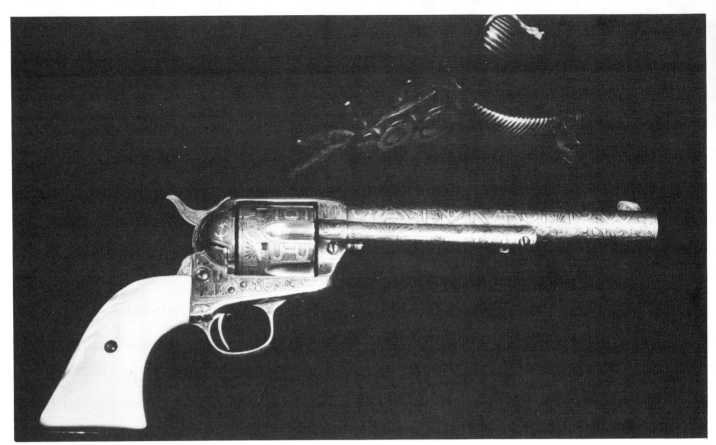

Serial No. 332139, .45 caliber Silver plated Colt, engraved with 58 early Texas Cattle Brands by the famous Texas gun engraver Cole Agee. Cole engraved only about 14 or 15 Colts with this pattern of engraving. Texas Rangers, early Texas Lawmen, and famous movie stars were among his clients.

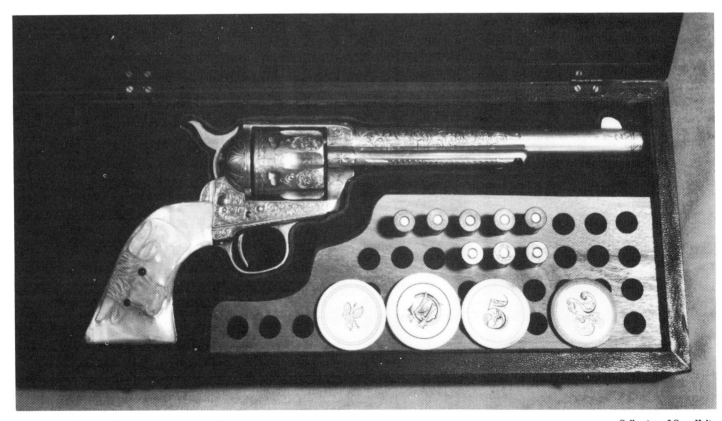

Serial No. 91692. 7 1/2" Colt .45: Shipped to Hartley and Graham June 7, 1883, engraved, carved steer head pearl grips, ruby eyes, silver plate finish.

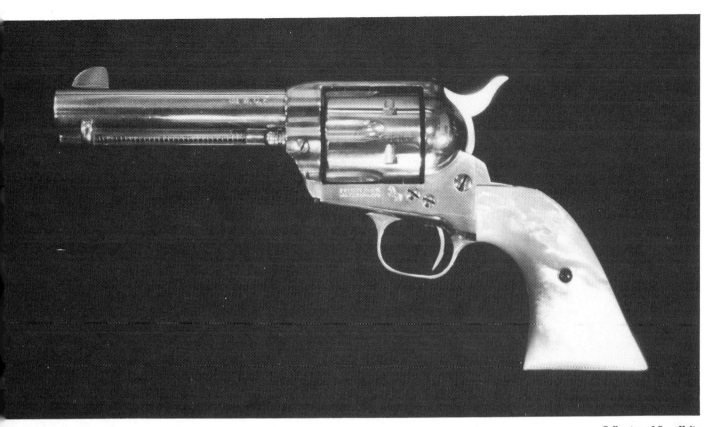

Collection of Gary Helin

Serial No. 345560. 4 3/4" Colt .38-40, nickel finish, pearl grips: Shipped to Simmon's Hardware, St. Louis, Missouri, April 19, 1923, c/o Ed Lindsey. Ed Lindsey served many years as a Texas Ranger starting in 1887 serving under Captain Frank Jones.

Ed Lindsey was born June 4, 1862, in Tupelo, Mississippi. Dennis Edward Lindsey was the only child of D. E. and Jennie Barnes Lindsey. His father was killed at the battle of Gettysburg while serving in the Confederate army and following his mother's remarriage Ed Lindsey left home in 1880.

Traveling alone by horseback, he first went to East Texas, where he had relatives, and opened a crossroads store. Lindsey's activities during the next few years cannot now be traced, but apparently he grew tired of the routine of life there. On February 15, 1887, he enlisted in Captain Frank Jones' Company D in Edwards County. His decision to become a Ranger may have been influenced by his cousin, Ben Lindsey, who was then a member of Captain Jones' company. He served at various points in South and Southwest Texas and was discharged in Duval County on May 31, 1888.

Collection of Gary Helin

Serial No. 296697. This .44-40 cal., 4 3/4" bbl., blue finish revolver was shipped directly to Mexico City July 6, 1907, to A. Combaluzier, a major dealer for Colt in old Mexico. The butt of the revolver is stamped Rep. of Mexico in bold type. Gun shows many years of hard use south of the border.

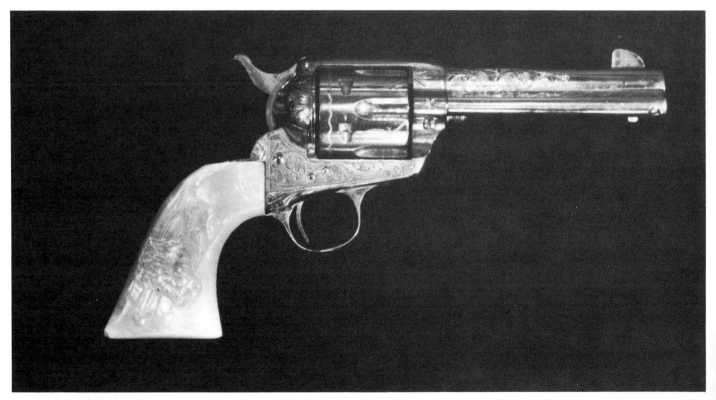

Collection of Gary Helin

Serial No. 327095. This .45 cal., 4 3/4" bbl., one-gun special order shipment, left Colt factory April 23, 1913. Sent to New Orleans, Louisiana, c/o O.H.A. Suuson. Factory engraved, nickel finish, carved steer head, mother of pearl grips. Gun was found in Western Kansas in the early 50's.

Serial No. 67897. 7 1/2" Colt .45, carved UTAH 1882 in right grip: This pistol was found in the desert in the early 40's buried in the sands of time.

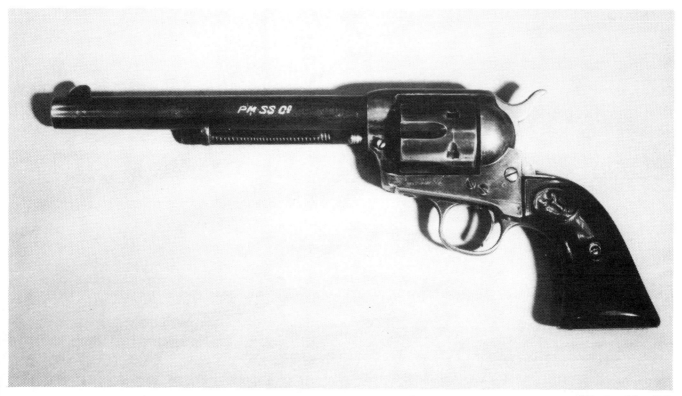

Serial No. 175937. 7 1/2" Colt .45, blue finish: Only known single action stamped P.M.S.S. Co. on left side of barrel.

Collection of Gary Helin

Serial No. 256515. Jack Case Colt. Quite a bit of interesting history has surfaced on Jack Case in the last few years. This gun and holster outfit was found in Reno, Nevada in the early 70's stored in an old trunk along with many of his personal effects. Jack Case owned and operated a Wild West Show for many years also starred in several early movies. This .38 Colt left the Colt factory July 4, 1904, c/o the Jackson Hughes Co., El Paso, Texas. Left triggerguard is stamped J. Case Shows.

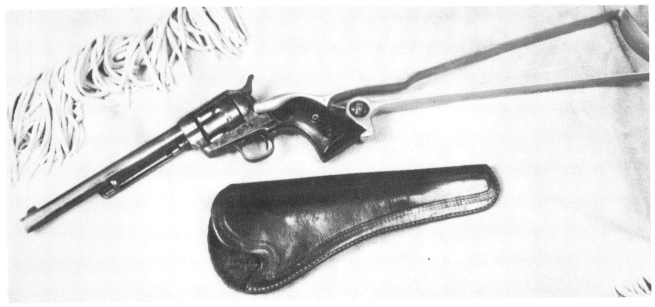

Collection of Gary Helin

Serial No. 97377. 8" Barrel .45 Colt, Blue Finish, hard rubber Eagle grips. Gun shows very good care, retaining 70% original blue finish. Also pictured is early California style 8" holster and factory attachable shoulder stock which theoretically converts this long-barreled Colt into a carbine.

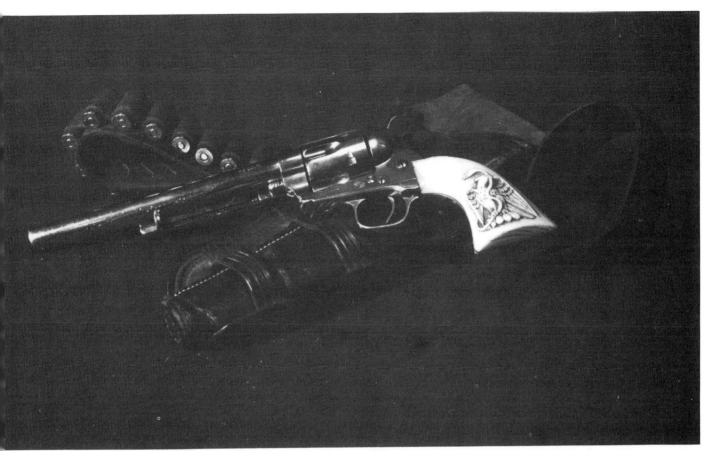

Serial No. 20816. Henry P. Purnell's Colt .45.

Collection of Gary Helin

Henry Purnell's father, Thomas Fassitt Purnell, was the first U.S. Marshal of Texas after the Civil War. Appointed by President Grant, Henry served as Deputy U.S. Marshal with his father in the 1870s and later served as Sheriff in Austin, Texas. This Colt .45 with his name inscribed on the backstrap was his personal weapon.

Collection of Gary Helin

Serial No. 21221. This 7 1/2" .45 Colt was purchased many years ago in Santa Fe, New Mexico from Mr. Harold Street. Street was given the Colt by an early Sheriff of Santa Fe. Gun shows much wear at the end of the barrel from many years of holster wear.

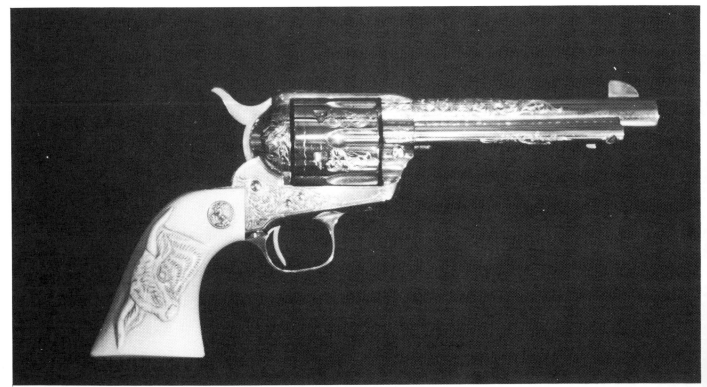

Collection of Gary Helin

Serial No. 354738. This .45 cal., full gold plated single action is one of a very few that will letter from Colt factory as finish - "full gold plate". Shipped to Abercrombie and Fitch, New York, February 19, 1932, special order No. 10959/1, one gun in shipment. Since Colt's total production in 1932 was only 300 guns and the great depression was in full swing, who would order a full gold plated Colt, factory engraved, such as this?

Collection of Gary Helin

Serial No. 55314, 7 1/2" Colt .44-40: This gun was purchased from descendants of the family of John Yates. Yates was in one of Custers Companies present at the Custer Battle. Right grip plate has wreath with initials J. Y. in center and dated 1876 to commemorate the year of the battle in Black Hills Gold.

Collection of Gary Helin

Serial No. 117652, Colt .44-40: Etched barrel silver plated with pearl grips, inscribed J. D. Shuford on left grip in black enamel. This gun was a special order one-gun shipment to Menges Hardware, Kansas City, Missouri, September 14, 1886.

Collection of Gary Helm

Serial No. 33235, Curly Bill, U.S.S.: This old tacked trunk contains the last possessions of Curly Bill, United States Scout. An old letter from an Army Officer found in the trunk dated March 14, 1905, Chickasha Indian Territory list his personal effects. These items were a U.S. bridle and bit, scout jacket and hat, Colt pistol and holster outfit, and gloves. The old Colt shows the signs of many years use on the plains. From the holster rig hangs the dial of an old pocket watch, a string of tube beads, and a lock of braided hair. Curly Bill was Chief of Scouts at Fort De Fiance and Fort St. Urain in Colorado.

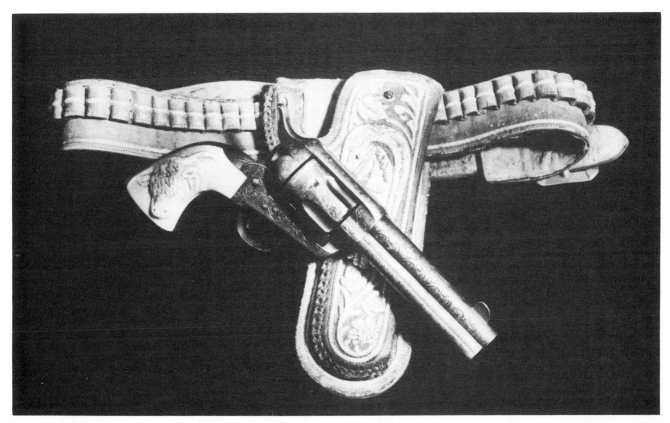

Collection of Gary Helin

Serial No. 217669. Colt .45 peacemaker, silver plated, engraved with ivory steer head grips: This gun was purchased from the estate of Eugene Kelner a South Dakota cowboy. He worked on the MacBeth ranch on Medicine Creek in South Dakota, later had his own spread, was considered a roving cowboy, with a short temper, a talent for playing the guitar, and could sing as good as Tom Mix. Kelner passed away in San Antonio, Texas in the early 40's.

Gene Kelner, 1903

Collection of Gary Heli

Serial No. 308107. Colt .32 W.C.F.: This old colt shows much use but very good care, retains 60% original blue finish engraved with pearl carved bull head grips. Produced in 1908, and pictured with turn of the century period style holster and tacked gunbelt.

W. M. Cauby jr.

The safety of the crews on the Choctaw, Oklahoma and Gulf railroad was in the hands of brave men armed with rapid fire pump shotguns like this 1893 Winchester. These early pump guns, although only suitable for black powder, were a great improvement in firepower over the older single and double barreled shotguns. Not many 1893s survive as Winchester recalled them when the 1897 model came out. If you sent in your 93' they sent you a 97' for free! The 93s were recycled into the furnace, hence their rarity.

The April Fool Colt

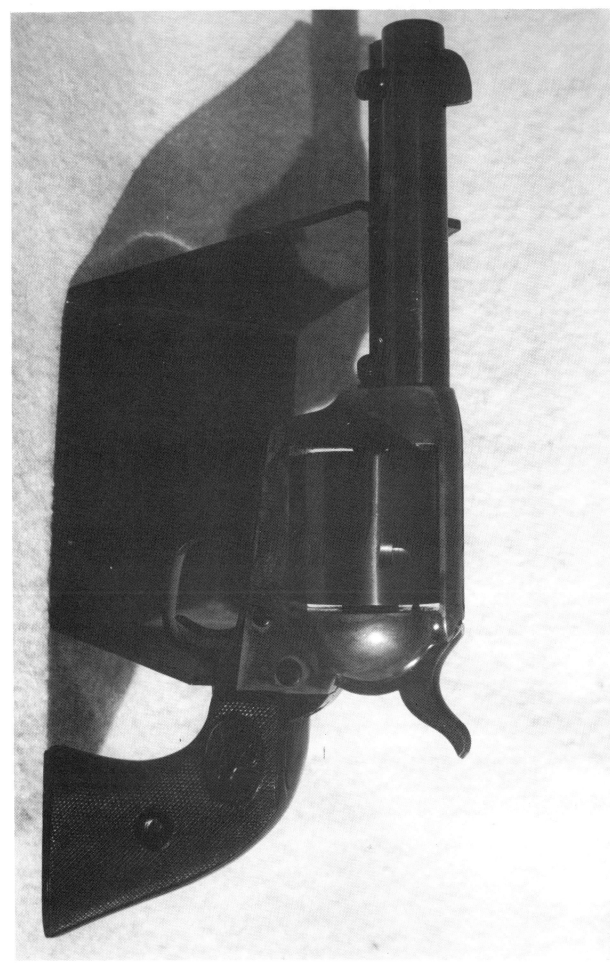

Collection of Mike Holloway

SN 35305I. This Colt was mfg. in 1929, .38-40, 4 3/4". 100% CC 99% Blue. A rare "somebody goofed" variation. It left the factory with the frame stamped with a sharp, well defined Rampant Colt but no patent dates (for further information refer to Kopec's book, *A Study of the Colt Single Action Army Revolver*, p. 179). Factory letter states "We have no explanation on the lack of patent dates on the frame of your firearm." Shipped to Denver CO 4-1-29. Was Colt playing April Fool with this one?

Collection of Mike Holloway

The Silverado Arvo Ojala Colts

From the personal collection of Hollywood's Legendary Gun Coach ARVO OJALA comes this pair of 4 3/4" barrel nickel plated .45LC COLT PEACEMAKERS SN SA51058 and SN SA26317 and his personal black double quick draw rig. These six-guns feature bent hammers for speed drawing, cocking and firing; lowered front sights; bevelled cylinders; Arvo's honed action. You saw these guns blazing across the screen in the hands of KEVIN COSTNER (Jake) in SILVERADO. Arvo's black double quick draw rig, HANDMADE BY ARVO HIMSELF, of tooled leather features: 20 cartridge loops; two fitted holsters; 20 silver plated non-firing cartridges; Arvo Ojala's name engraved inside of the belt in one-inch letters and an Arvo Ojala commemorative belt buckle. All this is documented by Arvo Ojala as well as photos taken on the set in New Mexico.

Arvo Ojala on SILVERADO movie set in New Mexico with Colt Peacemakers SA51058 and SA26317.

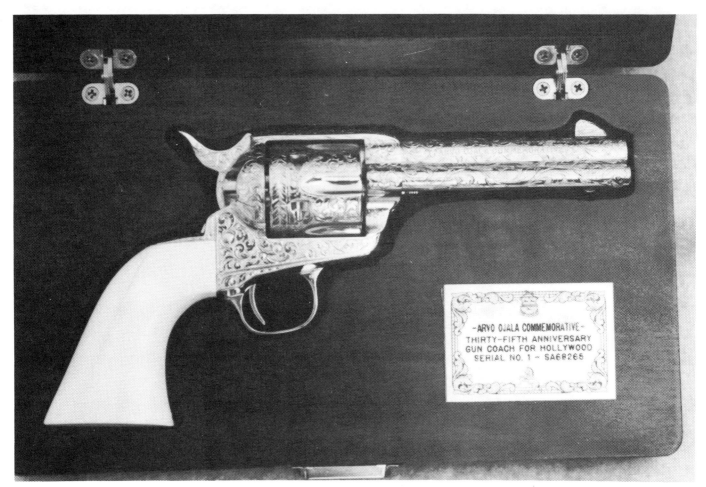

Collection of Mike Holloway

Arvo Ojala Commemorative Serial No. 1. 4 3/4 bbl., .45LC, 24K Gold Plated, full coverage engraved by Master Engraver, Robert Valade. This Colt SAA features Arvo's own customized hand worked action, bent hammer and one-piece ivory grips. This Colt Peacemaker commemorates Arvo's many contributions to the great Hollywood western movies. Arvo's work in "**Rustler's Rhapsody**," "**Silverado**," and "**Three Amigos**," which featured Arvo's fancy gun hand in action, are his most recent accomplishments. "Thirty-fifth anniversary gun coach for Hollywood No. 1" is inscribed on the back strap.

Collection of Mike Holloway

SN 170609. This fine condition .44-40 cal., 7 1/2" bbl., Colt Frontier Six Shooter, blue finish firearm was shipped May 11, 1897, to Hartley, Graham, New York, N.Y. shipment of three.

END OF HOLLOWAY COLLECITON

SN 163605. This magnificently factory engraved .45 cal., 4 3/4" bbl. left the Colt factory Dec. 20, 1895, for H. S. Bettes Hardware Co., Paris, Texas. According to factory records the firearm was factory engraved (From the Boys 1895) on backstrap. Finish silver, Pearl grips and shipment of one.

Private Collection

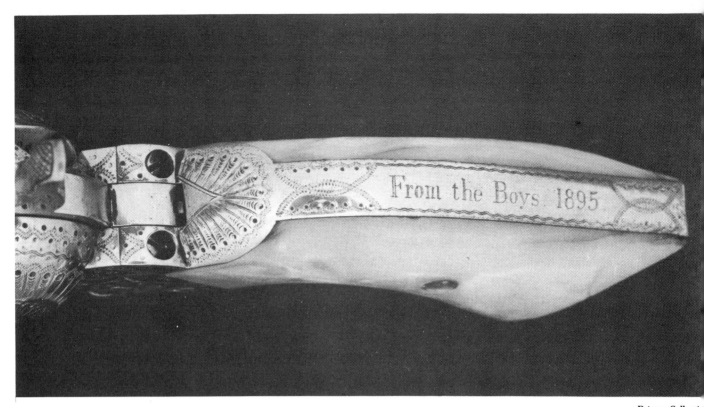

SN 163605. Backstrap View showing backstrap engraving "From the Boys 1895". This firearm was supposedly a gift for judge who served in Mt. Pleasant, Texas.

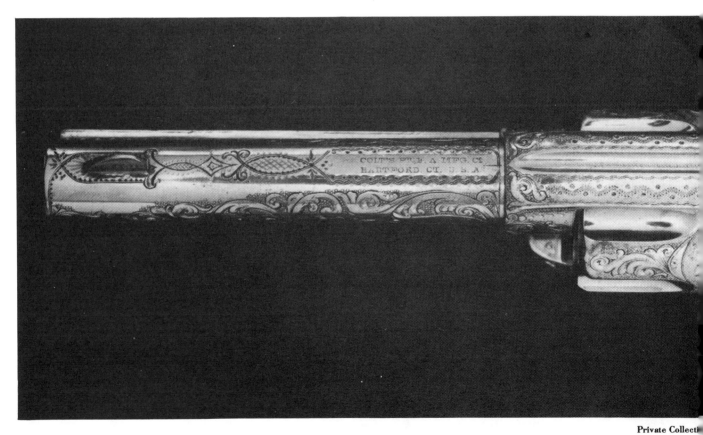

SN 163605. Top of Barrel View showing the unusually high grade of Helfricht engraving. Note the pattern extending to the top of the barrel.

SN 163605. Side View showing the fine quality engraving of Colt Master Engraver Cuno Helfricht. This could be the centerpiece of any book on firearms. Private Collection

Collection of Marshal Ralph L. Hooker

SN 89547. This .45 cal., 5 1/2" bbl., nickel finish was shipped April 6, 1883, to Hartley & Graham, New York, New York. It once belonged to St. Louis lawman James McDonough. Note the yellowed one-piece ivory grips.

James McDonough's SAA Colt

SN 89547. This .45 cal. was the property of James McDonough who operated a detective agency in the period of 1840 to late 1860. It is nickel plated with factory ivory grips. Mr. McDonough was the first chief of police in the city of St. Louis, Mo. accepting the post when it was established in 1861. He served five terms ending in 1884. The city of St. Louis and the police department purchased this gun and presented it to Mr. McDonough, who resigned in 1884. He carried this gun during his last term as chief of police. This gun was in storage on the west coast for many years, then obtained from Mr. McDonough's relatives.

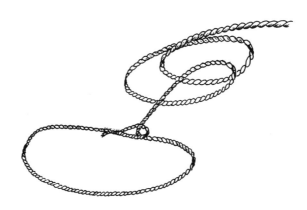

Portrait of J.R. Platt

A really handsome sidelock Continental 12 gauge double bbl. hammer shotgun, 30" damascus bbls., serial #21452.
On the rib it carries a gold inlay (shown above) "J R Platt Texas Rangers".
John R. Platt, also known as "Radd" or Rudd", served in Capt. Sam McMurray's Co. B of the Texas Rangers from 1886 to 1890.

Collection of Kurt House

SN 154018. This .45 cal., 4 3/4" bbl., nickel finish revolver with pearl grips was shipped December 6, 1893, to J. C. Petmecky, Austin, Texas especially for Texas Ranger Carl Kirchner. "Carl Kirchner" is inscribed underneath the barrel. Kirchner was a Texas Ranger from 1889 until 1895.

One of the truly great Rangers of the trans-Pecos area in the closing years of the nineteenth century was Carl Kirchner, who gained fame as a member of Company D.

He was born in Bee County, Texas, November 19, 1867, the son of Christian and Martha Burditt Kirchner, but was raised in Edwards County. Fulfilling an ambition of long standing, he became a Ranger May 18, 1889, and continued his long service until July 24, 1895, during which time he rose to the rank of First Sergeant in testimony of his efficiency. His entire service was in Southwest Texas, where he saw duty mainly at Ysleta, Shafter, Marfa, Pecos and Alpine. A participant in a number of gunfights, it is said he killed several men in the line of duty in experiencing great danger over an extended period.

Following his discharge he purchased and operated the Silver King Saloon in El Paso but within a short time sold the business to become a representative for a brewery.

On October 30, 1899, he married Mary Beck, his Edwards County sweetheart who became his devoted "Mamie." Following their marriage in San Antonio the Kirchners established residence in El Paso, where he was successful in business. There, their large home was the gathering place for many of his friends from Ranger days, especially his old comrade in arms Wood Saunders, with whom he had shared untold dangers.

Since he had made enemies on both sides of the Rio Grande, Kirchner usually went armed following his Ranger service, a practice he continued until his death. On at least one occasion this precaution appears to have saved his life. the incident occurred when he returned to Mexico to the scene of Captain Jones' death to witness the delivery of a large herd of horses and encountered several old enemies among the Mexicans there. So widespread was his reputation in that area as a "pistolero" that on one occasion in 1904 he was one of three men employed by the Mexican government to guard a shipment of money to Vera Cruz.

In 1911 he was a member of a group from El Paso who crossed the Rio Grande to Juarez to view the dead resulting from one of the numerous battles then being fought by opposing factions in Mexico. As the result of typhus contracted there the great Carl Kirchner died in El Paso on January 28, 1911. He is buried in the Concordia Cemetery in El Paso.

SN 154018. Underneath barrel view showing CARL KIRCHNER inscription.

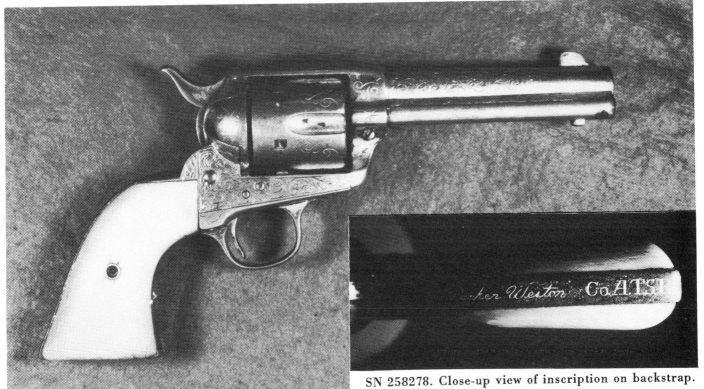

SN 258278. Close-up view of inscription on backstrap. Parker Weston, Co. A, T.S.R. The grips are ivory.

Collection of Kurt House

SN 258278. This .41 cal., 4 3/4" bbl., nickel, factory engraved revolver was shipped September 21, 1904, to H & D Folsom Arms Co., New York, New York. Shipment of one. This Colt was the sidearm of Texas Ranger Parker Weston. Parker served with Company A.

Parker Mayfield Weston was born October 27, 1882, at Richmond, Texas, the son of Dr. John M. Weston, a prominent physician and politician in Fort Bend County. Parker was named after J. Wesson Parker, Congressman from Fort Bend County in 1882 and Dr. John C. Mayfield who was a contemporary candidate for County Treasurer and good friend, perhaps business partner, of Dr. Weston's. Dr. Weston moved his family to Wilson County in 1889.

Actively recruiting Rangers in Wilson County was county resident Captain Will Wright, and his success can be measured by the Rangers that have originated from this county. It is probable.... that young Parker Weston developed his desire to become a Ranger from these events.

In 1901, Parker Weston enlisted as a Trumpeter in the Eighth U.S. Cavalry and was mustered out March 8, 1904, the year that Colt Number 258278 was specially ordered from the Colt Factory by Folsom Arms Company. On the 9th of July of that year he promptly enlisted in the Texas National Guard at Houston, Texas, and it was about a year later that his "Cowboy Portrait" was taken with his engraved ivory-handled Colt Single Action and his "Gal Leg Spurs". In 1906, due no doubt to Captain Wright's influence, Parker joined the Ranger service on October 8, three weeks before his real twenty-fourth birthday. Parker was issued a 1907 Winchester while in Ranger service, and his daughter remembers his scout belt, as he explained the difference in the .41 Colt cartridges and the larger rifle cartridges.

By 1917, Parker had retired from the hard west Texas life of a Texas Ranger and was hired as a security guard for the then-fledgling Texas Oil Company which later became Texaco.

Parker, who was now a pumper at Sour Lake, Texas, died from pneumonia the night of July 22, 1936.

PARKER WESTON
Photo taken about 1905 near Houston, Texas.

SA 91670. This .45 cal., 5 1/2" bbl. revolver was shipped June 9, 1883, to Simmons Hardware Co., St. Louis, Missouri. This was the service revolver of Special Texas Ranger J. E. "Ed" Russell. (see story below)

Collection of Kurt House

Special Ranger J. E. Russell was born at Blum, Hill County, Texas, in December, 1873. He had the traditional Ranger physical characteristics: six feet one inches tall, 205 pounds, dark complexioned and blue eyes. While not much is known of his adolescence, his father, John Russell was a Captain in the Confederacy and was the first mayor of Mesquite, Texas. His photograph is currently in the Mesquite City Hall, a bearded likeness of his son.

In 1889, Ed's father had served as a cavalryman with Pershing during his chase of Pancho Villa. Ed moved to Dallas and was elected Justice of the Peace for Precinct 4 (Oak Cliff) in 1912.

About this time he relocated to the town of Matador in Motley County where he served two years as Deputy Sheriff. He was subsequently elected Sheriff, and after serving for twelve years, first took the Ranger oath of service in Austin on April 30, 1926. He was married, listed as a stock-farmer, and had one year's experience as Inspector for the Texas and Southwestern Cattle Raiser's Association. His Ranger Warrant of Authority shows his residence at Matador, and that he was appointed Special Ranger at the request of the Texas and Southwestern Cattle Raiser's Association. Probably the huge Matador Ranch, managed by the Campbell family was both the reason for his appointment and his jurisdiction.

Matador Ranch historian Harry Campbell records in his book *The Early History of Motley County* (1958) that Ranger Russell was one of the best peace officers in the state, possessing a "natural instinct for ferreting out the criminal that defied explanation...". Russell solved difficult crimes without apparent clues, seeming to rely on "...an inbred sense of suspicion..." toward the guilty. Suspecting arson in a fire that almost destroyed the town of Roaring Springs, he visited the scene, singled out a suspect and the investigation which followed proved him right. When the Matador drug store was robbed, he kept surveillance on two boys until one day while watching them from the court house cupola with field glasses, he followed them to where they had buried the loot. In another instance, the depot in Matador was burglarized and abstracts of Campbell's entire ranch were stolen, among other things. Ranger Russell and Robert Meddlin recovered the stolen materials in the brush without a single clue.

Ranger Ed Russell was elected Dallas County Treasurer in 1924, and ran again in 1928. The Dallas Times Herald issue of February 22, 1927, shows a photo attesting the integrity of Ed Russell; it pictures him accepting as county treasurer, a check from the county tax collector for over one million dollars.

According to his grandson, during the period that Ed Russell was county treasurer and simultaneously a Ranger, he officed down at Fair Park which was Company B commanded by Captain Tom Hickman. Russell's grandson, an eyewitness to the facts, also explains that his grandfather kept two Colt Single Actions; a worn blue one for every day use, then had his favorite .45 nickel plated and used it as his "parade" gun. Old Colt #91, 670 was shipped from Colt to Simmons Hardware in 1883, just six years before Ed's father joined the cavalry. Russell retired from Ranger service in 1936.

Ed Russell had four daughters and one son. In 1937, he again entered politics, running for City Council Place 1 (South Oak Cliff), where his sole surviving daughter (Margaret Wilson, born 1900) still resides. After serving his city, county, and state for almost fifty years, Ed Russell died on Memorial Day 1945, and was buried in Grove Hill Cemetery in Dallas, Texas. (From *Texas Ranger Sketches* 1972 Robert W. Stephens)

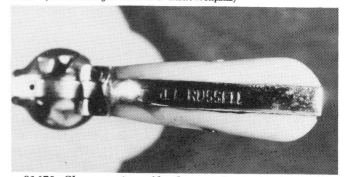

91670. Close-up view of backstrap showing inscription, "J. E. Russell."

Original Tintype of Jim Putnam

Winchester 1886 lever action, 45-70 cal., serial #4892, engraved on the receiver is;"James M. Putnam Company D Frontier Battalion Texas Rangers". Putnam served in the Texas Rangers from June 1, 1890 until July 22 1893. He distinguished himself on January 31, 1891 in a gunfight with the wanted killer Fine Gilliland. Putnam and his partner, Thalis Cook followed Gilliland into the Glass Mountains just north of Marathon. Upon being confronted by the two Rangers, Gilliland wounded Cook and killed his horse. As Gilliland was attempting to flee, Putnam shot the outlaw's horse dead with his 45-70. Taking refuge behind his fallen steed, Gililand raised his head to take aim at the rangers. That proved a fatal mistake as Putnam's 45-70 roared again and Gilliland took the fatal slug through the head.

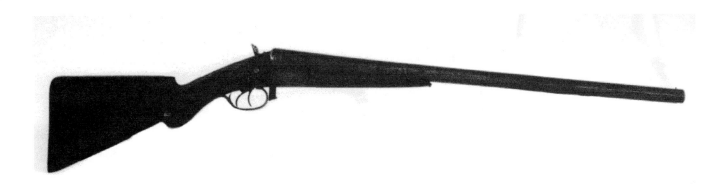

This very early Parker Bros. underlifter 10 gauge presentation shotgun has 30" damascus bbls. It is serial #7718 and is engraved on the top rib "Presented to Marshall Jesse L. Hall from the Grateful Citizens of Sherman Texas". To have been presented such a fine gun, the lawman must have done something exceptional for his town and its people. After serving as the town Marshall, he later became a Texas Ranger.

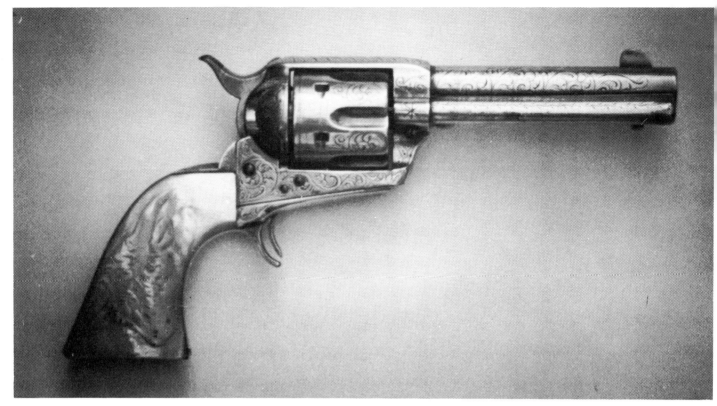

Collection of Lee Hutcheson

SN 235590. Colt records confirm this .45 cal., 4 3/4" bbl. revolver was factory engraved, silver finished, and shipped January 16, 1903, to Walter Tips, Austin, Texas. The beautiful carved steerheads are noted in the factory letter. Records make no mention of the cut-off trigger guard.

Senator Walter Earnest Tips
Texas Leader

In the period when the Texas of today was still an unrealized dream and hope of the future, Senator Walter Ernest Tips rose to prominence in the life of the State, and by the actual worth of his accomplishments contributed much to its progress. He became the greatest wholesale and retail merchant in Texas, a builder of vast civic enterprises and a leader in all projects for the benefit of his city and State in this great period of development. He won the admiration and respect of all, and his name today is assured a lasting remembrance in the ranks of those who may truthfully be called builders of the Texas empire.

Senator Tips was born at Elberfeld on the Rhine, in Germany, on July 23, 1841, a son of Conrad and Caroline (Braun) Tips. His father was a man of prominence in Elberfeld, serving as city secretary and taking an active part in city and governmental affairs. Because of the restrictions of the German Government and the strife which they engendered, he came to America with his family soon after the Revolution of 1848, settling at Seguin, Texas, where he died.

Walter Ernest Tips, of this record, received his educational training in the public schools. After his father's death, he was able to attend school only a little, but he was an insatiable student, and in the evenings, or in his hours of leisure, carried on his reading and studies. He mastered the various aspects of human knowledge and became familiar with the best literature of the world. In addition, from his earliest years he proved himself a talented musician, and as a boy would practice nights in the back of the little store where he worked, learning to play upon the violin and later upon the cello, which was his favorite instrument. Senator Tips began his independent business career at New Braunfels, where he established a general mercantile business with two partners. Later he came to Austin, Texas, and purchased his brother's business in this city, his earlier partners still being interested with him in this venture. Senator Tips immediately converted the store into a general hardware enterprise, and within a few years became sole owner of the business. Under his able guidance the volume of its trade steadily increased, and Senator Tips soon became known as a foremost man of business in the State. With his vast powers of intellect and his knowledge of the lessons which history alone can teach, he also became a leader in every phase of State affairs, not only commercial, but educational, civic, and social. He was an intellectual giant, broad of mind and vision.

Collection of Lee Hutcheson

N 338927. This .44-40 cal., 5 1/2" bbl., blue finish Colt Frontier Six Shooter was shipped April 1, 1920, to Momsen, Dunigan, Ryan Co., El Paso, Texas. Shipment of five. Shown with old contemporary studded holster & belt.

Collection of Lee Hutcheson

N 154205. This rare "sheriff's model" .45 cal., nickel finish with carved pearl steerhead on left side left the Colt Factory July 1894, bound for Turner Hardware Co., Muskogee, (Indian Territory) Oklahoma. Shipment of one. The Factory letter cites the 4" bbl. shown here with an early U. S. Deputy Marshal Indian Territory Crescent over Star badge.

Collection of Lee Hutcheson

SN 123708. This Smith & Wesson model 1905 revolver was the personal sidearm of Harry Puryear, Sheriff, Chaves County, New Mexico during the 1950s. Note the inscription on the frame in photo. Also shown are Sheriff Puryear's badges and handcuffs.

Certificate of Election, Chaves County, New Mexico

Collection of David Janousek

SN 143930. This .41 cal., 4 3/4" bbl., nickel finish revolver was manufactured in 1891 and was used by Coal County, Oklahoma Sheriff Thea Bonner. Bonner was sheriff from 1927 until 1972.

Collection of David Janousek

SN 249295. This .32-20 cal., 4 3/4" bbl., was manufactured in 1903 and is shown here with a beautiful S. D. Myers, El Paso, Texas double-loop holster & belt. The upper full-flap holster and belt are unmarked. Also in photo is an early Indian Territory badge.

EL PASO PHOTO TAKEN IN 1891
Bernard Thorner and his wife, Bertha, are pictured here with son, Eugene. The photo was taken in El Paso, Texas, in 1891. The Colt in photo is serial # 138380, & .44-40 cal. with 7 1/2" bbl. (photo courtesy of Great Grandson William T. Goodman.)

Colt third model derringer, also known as the "Thuer". It's a 41 caliber rimfire with a 2&1/2 bbl, serial #18558. It served as a hideaway backup gun for Wells Fargo special agent and "G Man" Howard Dustin Pulsifer, whose photograph is shown at right.

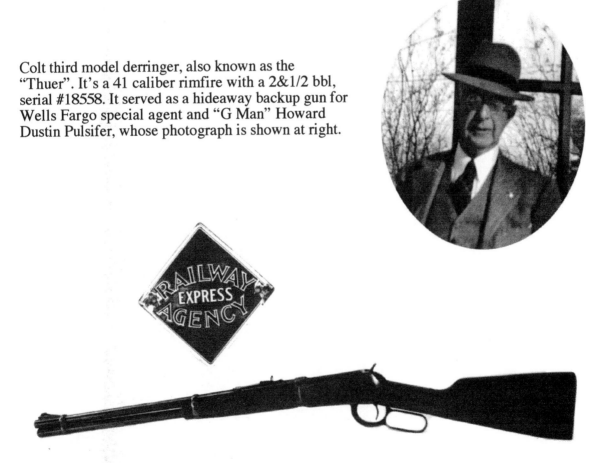

This rifle is a Winchester model 1894 in 30-30 caliber, serial #2192005. It is marked as the property of the Railway Express Agency on the receiver. It was probably used as a guard's rifle for protecting shipments or REA buildings.

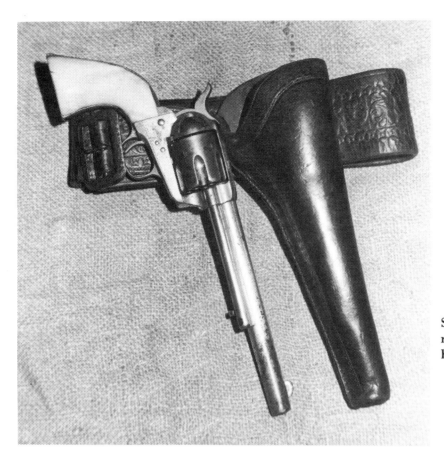

Collection of Bob Lar[...]
SN 43135. .45 cal. no record mfg. 1878, 7 1/2[...] nickel ivory grips with California "Slim Jim[..."] holster with engraved money belt.

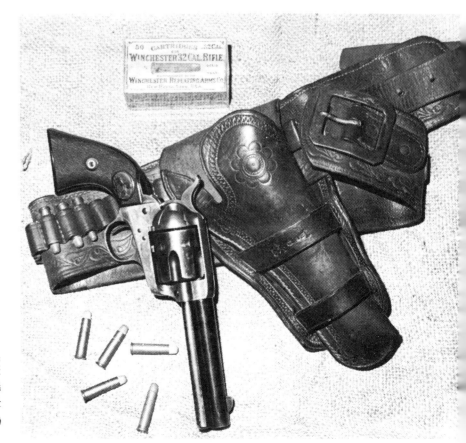

Collection of Bob Lan[...]
SN 201752. .32 WCF, 4 3/4" blue shipped Nov. 13, 1900, to Roberts, Sanford & Taylor Co., Sherman, Texas with "OLIVE" marked holster and money belt.

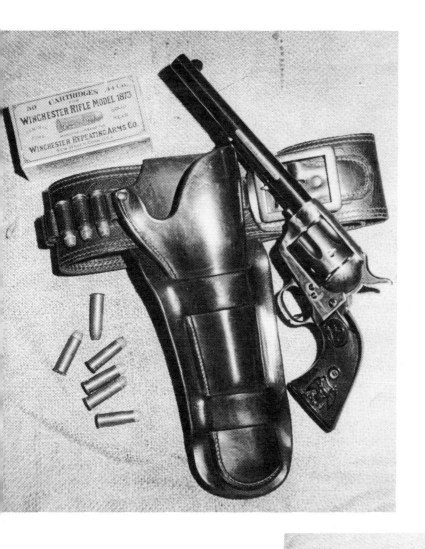

Collection of Bob Land

SN 105957. .44 WCF etched panel 7 1/2" blue, shipped to Manzanares & Co., Las Vegas, New Mexico (territory) April 1, 1887, (mfg. 1884) with Hieser Holster & money belt.

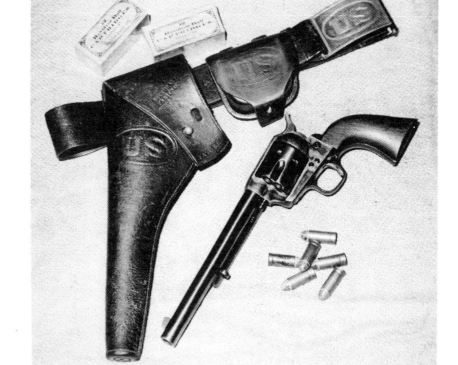

Collection of Bob Land

SN 61927 U. S. Calvary .45 cal. shipped to U. S. Govt. at Colt Factory in 1880. Inspected by David F. Clark with 1874 belt, cartridge pouch & 1881 holster.

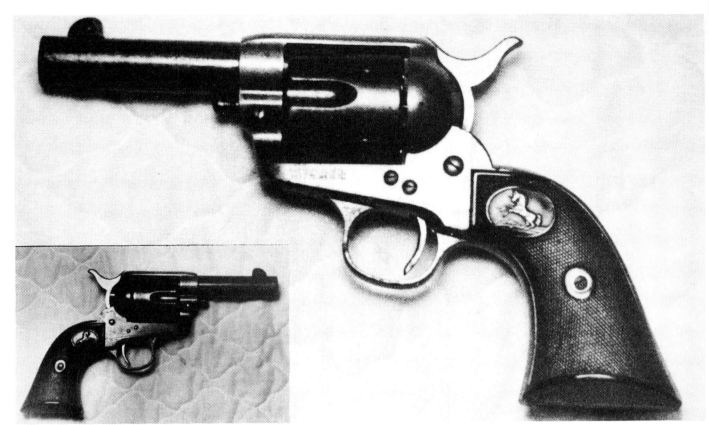

Collection of Bob Lane

SN 198313. This .45 cal., 3 1/2" bbl., blue finish rare Storekeeper's or Sheriff's Model was shipped September 27, 1901, to Simmon's Hardware Co., St. Louis, Missouri, o/o W.M.C. Hill. This Colt was carried by Feltus Ogden Swan, U.S. Border Patrol in McAllen, Texas. Current research may show this rare Colt to have Texas Ranger association.

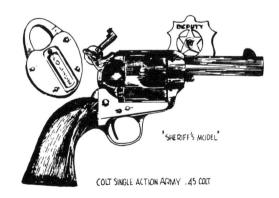

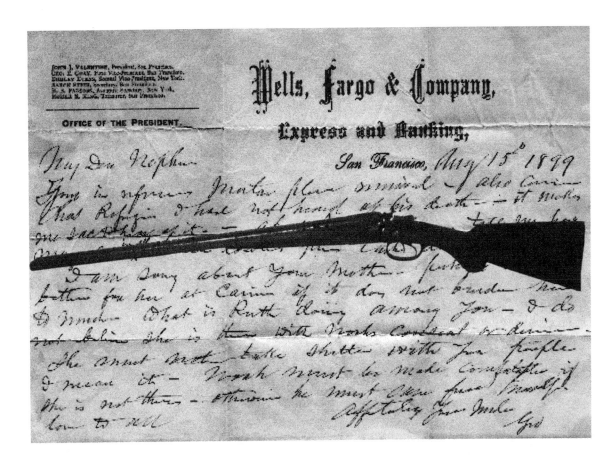

This Parker 12 gauge double barrel hammer double shotgun was owned by George E. Gray, the First Vice President of Wells Fargo & Company Express. It is shown overlaid on a letter from Mr. Gray to his nephew. It is believed that the shotgun, monogrammed G.E.G. on the trigger guard and W.F. & Co. on the silver shield on the wrist, came into the nephew's possession at some later date. A very nice old Parker with an unusual connection to one of America's most famous express companies.

An original W.F.& Co. franked envelope to be used over the Well fargo network. Finding an unused one is every collectors dream.

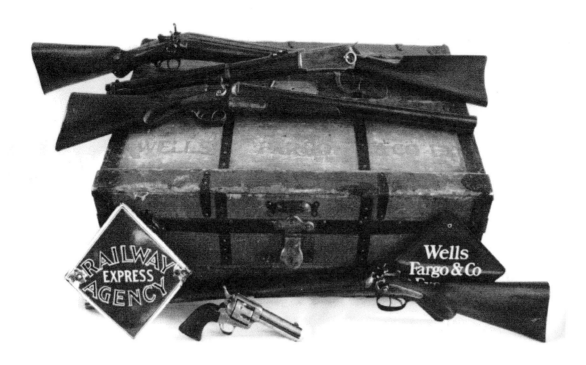

Shown atop a company shipping trunk is a group of Wells Fargo & Company Express guns. They are from top to bottom; a Saxton 12 ga double serial # 2815, a Winchester 1894 saddle ring carbine in 38-55 serial #45432, a J. Manton & Co. 10 gauge double bbl., serial #1274, a Nouman Bros. 12 ga double bbl., serial #27 and a Colt SAA in 44-40 caliber. All the guns carry markings identifying them as Wells Fargo property. In addition the SAA, marked WF & CO on the butt, also is engraved on the backstrap; H.D."Guns"Pulsifer.
Howard Dustin Pulisfer was a Wells Fargo special agent and a U.S. government "G Man".

An original photo of an early W.F.& Co. express man.

Two dudes dressed up as W.F.& Co. agents in a studio setting.

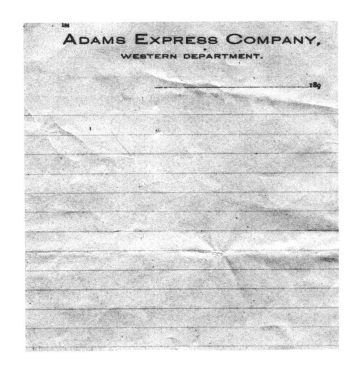

Philo J. Andersen

This E. James & Co. 12 gauge double barreled shotgun, serial #6669 was used to guard the valuables of The Adams Express Company by trusted guards such as the man shown above. Adams was one of the many competitors with Wells Fargo. Shown with the gun are Adams Express note paper and their own envelope with an embossed and colored logo.

Buffalo Bill's Wild West Show was famous entertainment from 1883 to 1916. This type of canvas banner would have been used to announce the show's attractions to the potential customers.

This unusual and rare shotgun was manufactured by the Union Firearms Company of Toledo Ohio. It is a hammerless pump gun, 12 gauge with a 30" damascus bbl. with a raised solid rib. The company was only in business from 1903-13 at which time its assets were purchased by the Ithaca Gun Company. This gun, serial #5725 is marked "Buffalo Bill's Wild West Show" on the tang. It was probably used for exhibition shooting at glass balls with very fine shot known as dust shot.

These are two interesting images from postcards of Buffalo Bill. In the one on the left he appears quite a bit older than the other. It may have been made near the end of his career. In spite of the burden of the years, he still projected a magnificent presence.

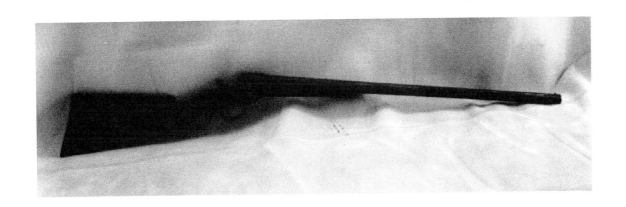

This Hopkins & Allen single barrel shotgun was used by the Indian police at the Wind River Agency in the Wyoming Territory to keep the native peoples in bondage. This unpleasant work was carried out under the direction of U.S. Government appointed agents such as the dour individual shown at the left.

While this oppression of the Native Americans was taking place, folks back east were being fed the propaganda of the noble savages as portrayed in the two post card photos at the bottom of the page. These 19th century beauties bore little resemblance to the women of the tribes living on the agencies meager subsistence rations and in barely adequate shelter.

Collection of Ben Powell

SN 182179. This .38-40 cal., 4 3/4" bbl., blue finish revolver was manufactured in 1899. According to documents accompanying this Peacemaker it was used by a McClennen County, (Waco) Texas lawman around the turn of the century. No factory record is available. Shown with a Mexican-style single-loop holster & belt.

Collection of Ben Powell

SN 193124. This .38-40 cal., 4 3/4", factory engraved Bisley revolver left the Colt factory, February 22, 1900, bound for Hibbard, Spencer & Bartlett, Chicago, IL. The Carved Pearl Eagle grips were probably added by the dealer.

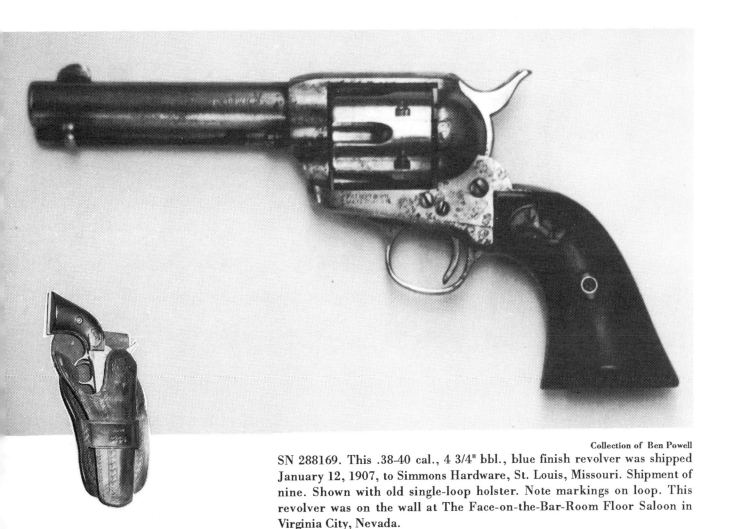

Collection of Ben Powell

SN 288169. This .38-40 cal., 4 3/4" bbl., blue finish revolver was shipped January 12, 1907, to Simmons Hardware, St. Louis, Missouri. Shipment of nine. Shown with old single-loop holster. Note markings on loop. This revolver was on the wall at The Face-on-the-Bar-Room Floor Saloon in Virginia City, Nevada.

Face-on-the-Bar-Room Floor Colt SAA

August 23, 1980

To Whom it May Concern:

In early June of this year, I heard about an auction to be held in Carson City—all items auctioned were from the "Face-on-the-Bar-Room Floor Saloon" in Virginia City, Nevada.

Being a resident of this area and having "put in a bit of elbow time" at this bar, I went to the auction and obtained a Colt Peacemaker #288169, caliber .38-40, which had been hanging behind the bar. Most of the items hanging on the walls were there because they had been traded for a bottle of liquor or a few dollars for a night on the town. Practically all the items were obtained in the early 1900's. I personally know that this particular Colt has been there since 1953.

The auction house that disposed of the items is Pasadena Auction Galleries, 77 No. Raymond Avenue, Pasadena, California 91103, Fred Clark, Auctioneer. This Colt was item B-19.

Sincerely,

Jim Butler

END OF POWELL COLLECTION

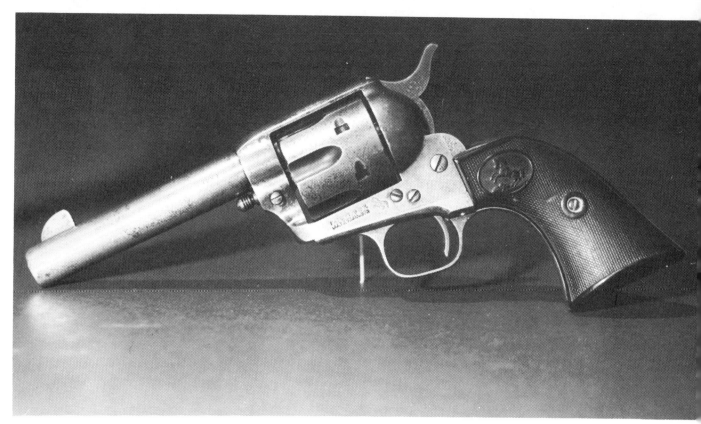

SN 347834. Factory records show this .45 cal., blue finish revolver was shipped *without an ejector rod!*. It was shipped February 8, 1927, to C. L. Bering, Houston, Texas. shipment of one. This is a rare 4 3/4" barrel store-keeper's model. The Bering-Cortez hardware store was destroyed by fire in approximately 1925. Cortez was a brother-in-law to C. L. Bering.

Collection of L. A. Rich,

SN 347834. Right side view showing ejectorless sheriff's model.

Collection of L. A. Rich,

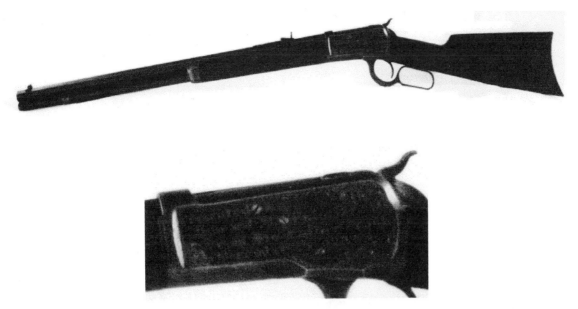

Winchester 1892 lever action rifle, 24" octagon bbl., 44-40 cal, serial #31612, Engraved on the receiver is "Presented to Howard D. Pulsifer from his Farther Frank December 25, 1894. A memorable Christmas gift from a Civil War hero, Frank H. Pulsifer, to his son , a Wells Fargo Special Agent and "G Man".

A very early rare LeFever presentation 10 gauge double bbl. shotgun. 31&1/4" damascus bbls., serial #9249, Inlaid silver shield in buttstock is engraved "Delazon LaFever In Appreciation Daniel M. LeFever".

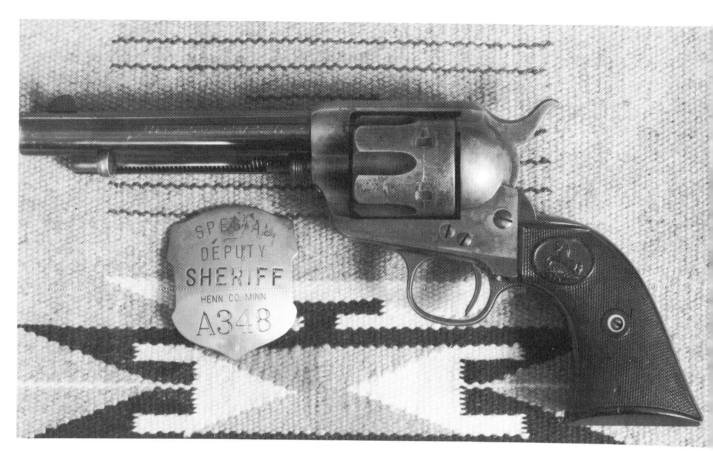

SA 146298. This .44-40 cal., 5 1/2" bbl., blue finish Colt Frontier Six Shooter was shipped May 23, 1892, to C. W. Hacket Hardware Co., St. Paul, Minnesota. Shipment of five. The rubber stocks are original.

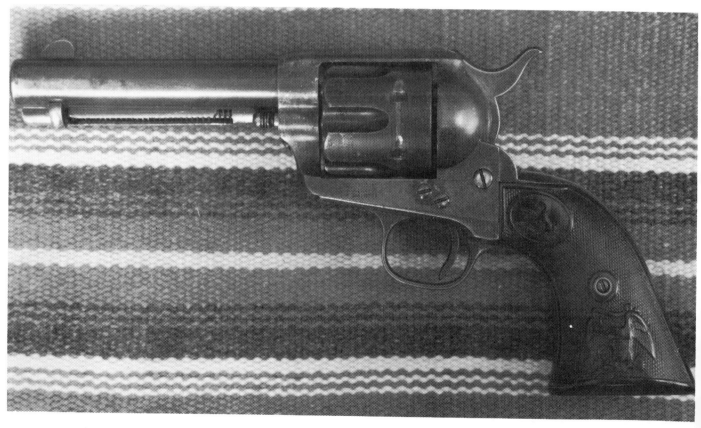

SN 129647. This .41 cal., 4 3/4" bbl., blue finish revolver was shipped August 16, 1889, to Colt's Agency, San Francisco, California. Shipment of five.

SN 350865. This .45 cal., 4 3/4" bbl., blue finish revolver was shipped December 21, 1927, to the City of San Antonio Police Department, San Antonio, Texas. Shipment of fifty. "S.A.P.D. 142" is factory engraved on butt.

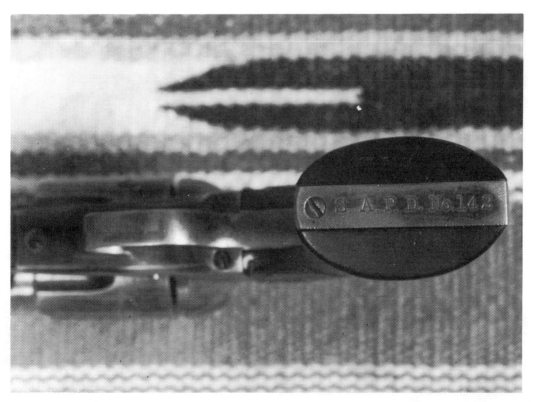

SN 350865. Butt View showing factory markings. The butt numbers in this shipment consisted of S.A.P.D. 101 through 150.

Collection of Ike Robert

SN 121632. This .45 cal., 4 3/4" bbl., blue finish revolver with eagle hard rubber grips was shipped August 19, 1887, Manzanares & Co., Las Vegas, New Mexico Territory. Fifty in shipment. This revolver has most of the original fini remaining.

Collection of Ike Robert

SN 273813. This .38-40 cal., 5 1/2" bbl., blue finish revolver was shipped February 13, 1906, to Thomson Diggs Hardw: Company, Sacramento, California. shipment of three.

Collection of Ike Robertson

SN 121465. This .44-40 cal., 7 1/2" bbl., blue finish Colt Frontier Six-Shooter etched panel was shipped May 5, 1887, to William Beck & Sons, Portland, Oregon. Shipment of six. The nice Eagle grips are original.

Collection of Ike Robertson

SN 122236. This .45 cal., 5 1/2" bbl., blue finish revolver was shipped June 17, 1887, to Clabrough & Golcher, San Francisco, California. Shipment of three. Note the original Walnut stocks.

SN 142593. This rare .38 cal., 4 3/4" bbl., blue finish revolver was shipped September 2, 1891, to Babcock & Miles, Red Lodge, Montana. Shipment of three. The Eagle grips are original.

SN 142509. It is always interesting to find two guns in the same shipment. This .38 cal., 4 3/4" bbl., blue finish revolver was in the same shipment to Red Lodge, Montana, as the above revolver.

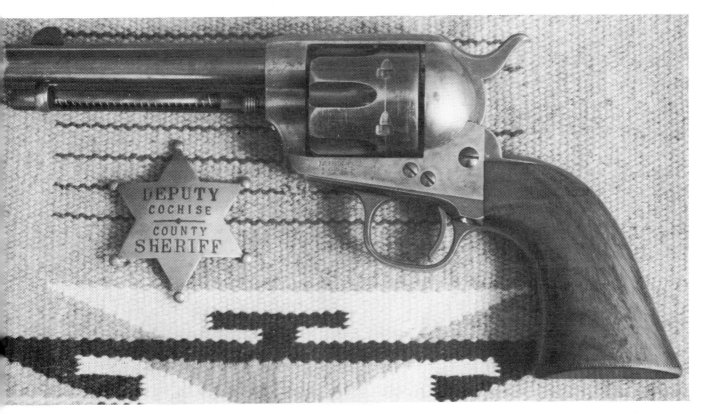

Collection of Ike Robertson

N 121569. This .44-40 cal., 4 3/4" bbl., blue finish Colt Frontier Six Shooter etched panel was shipped April 6, 1887, to Manzanares & Co., Las Vegas, New Mexico (Territory) Shipment of one-hundred. The one-piece Walnut stocks are original to this Colt.

END OF ROBERTSON COLLECTION

Francisco A. Manzanares

Francisco A. Manzanares was born at Abiquiu, New Mexico, on January 25, 1843. It is interesting to note that he was one of the few native sons of New Mexico and one of the better known citizens of Las Vegas to make the "All-Time Popularity" list. His father, Jose Antonio, gave him his early education. He was then sent to Taos to Padre Martinez's school.

Francisco first entered business in New York where he graduated from school; then Kansas. In 1864 he returned to New York where he worked as a teller in a New York bank.

In 1879 he opened two stores in Socorro and Las Vegas. Lawrence B. Browne was his partner and the firm was known as Browne & Manzanares. The business expanded so rapidly that in 1885 it was found expedient to organize a stock company. Browne & Manzanares were the founders of the Las Vegas Water Company, the First National Bank of Las Vegas, and several enterprises. Manzanares served as delegate to the United States Congress from New Mexico. In 1871 he married Antonia Baca. Lawrence Browne died in December, 1893, but the firm continued to use both the names. Manzanares, New Mexico, is named after Francisco and Jose Antonio Manzanares.

from "The Las Vegas Story" by F. Stanley

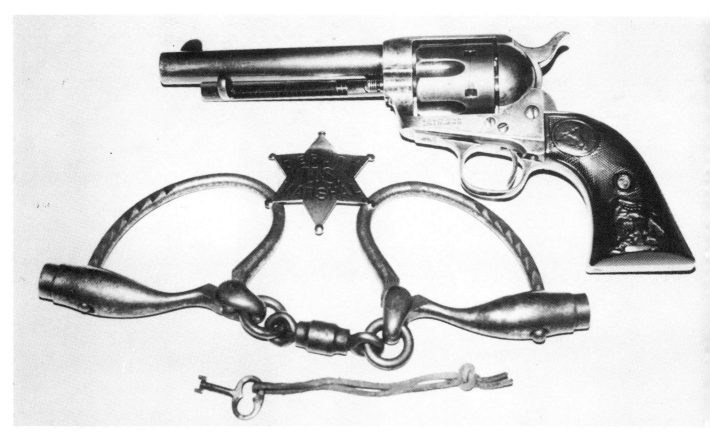

Photo by G. R. Taylor   Collection of Robert Schubert
SN 142678. This .45 cal. 5 1/2" bbl. blue finish revolver was shipped Oct. 2, 1891 to Dunlay & Geisler, Houston, Texas. Shipment of three. Note the eagle grips.

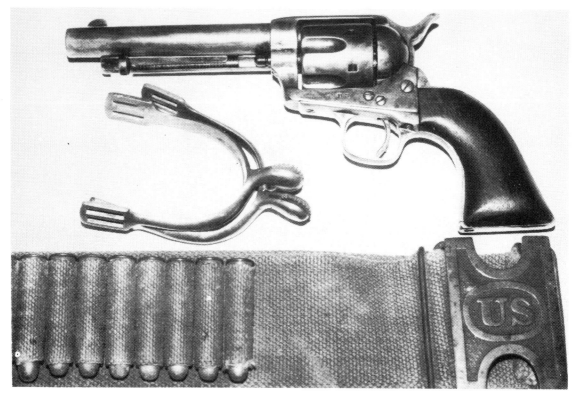

Photo by G. R. Taylor   Collection of Robert Schubert
SN 5041. This U. S. Artillery .45 cal. 5 1/2" firearm was originally shipped to the United States Government with a 7 1/2" bbl. It was returned to the factory for cleaning, refinishing, and the barrel was cut to 5 1/2". It was shipped Jan. 29, 1902, to the Springfield Armory, Springfield, Mass. Shipment of fifty.

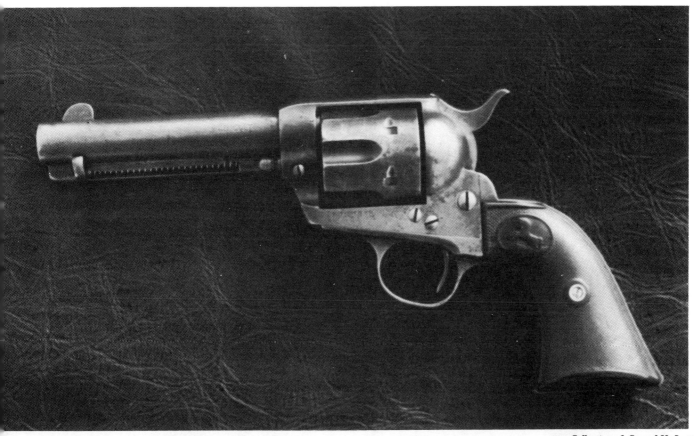

Collection of Conard M. Scott

N 281716. This .45 cal., 4 3/4" bbl., blue finish revolver was shipped August 29, 1906, to Walter Tips Company, Austin, Texas. Shipment of ten.

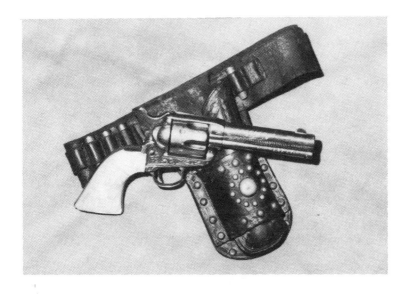

DR. JOHN R. COLLINS. This photo was probably taken in Nowata, Oklahoma shortly after the turn of the century. Collins was a prominent physician in the Oklahoma area. He died in 1929 at the age of 50. Obviously, Dr. Collins is very proud of the weapons he is displaying.

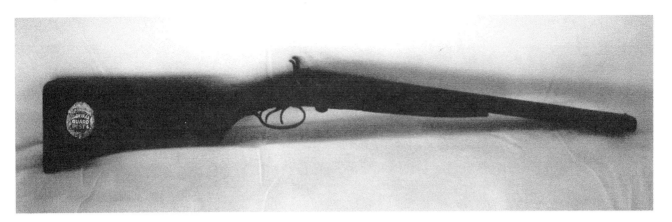

Wm. Moore & Co. 12 gauge double bbl. hammer shotgun with 20" bbls., serial #2538.

This gun served as a guard shotgun at the famous Federal prison on Alcatraz island in San Francisco bay.

An enlarged photograph of the badge attached to the buttstock.

A Batavia Leader 12 gauge double barrel shotgun with 28" damascus bbls., serial #101149 This is a presentation shotgun and was given to A.W. Johnston by the Lake Shore & Southern Michigan Railway Company. The presentation is beautifully engraved on the sideplate of the lock. An fascinating item of American railroad history.

Collection of Charles Schreiner, III

SN 343205 (upper). This .45 cal., 5 1/2" bbl., nickel finish revolver was shipped Jan. 28, 1922, to Praeger Hardware, San Antonio, Texas. The lower .45 cal., 5 1/2" bbl., nickel finish revolver SN 343343 was shipped Aug. 21, 1922 to Wolf and Klar, Fort Worth, Texas. Note the beautiful carved steerhead grips and unusual medallions on these revolvers.

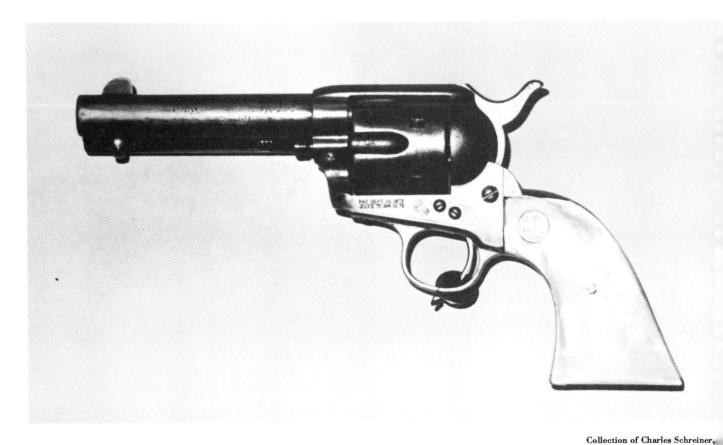

Collection of Charles Schreiner,

SN 189743. This .45 cal., 4 3/4" bbl. revolver with pearl grips was used by J. T. Flournoy (1902-1982). He served with t Fayette County, Texas sheriff's department in 1929, and became a Texas Ranger in 1941. Flournoy was from La Grange, Texa

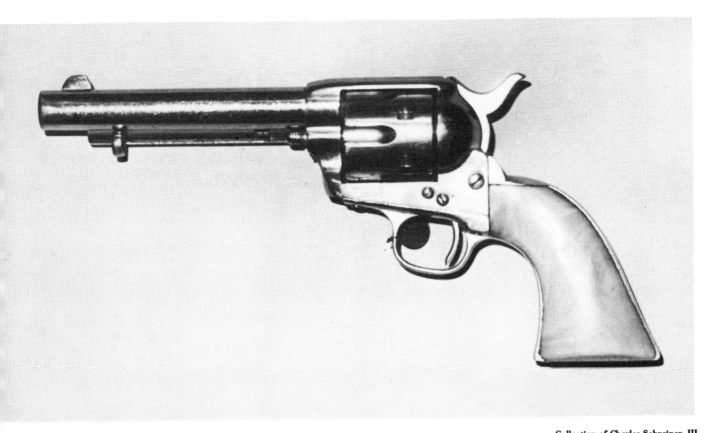

SN (none). This .45 cal., 5 1/2" bbl., nickel finish revolver was manufactured prior to 1898 and was owned and used by Texas Ranger John Horan, Mason, Texas around 1914. Note the nice one-piece ivory grips.

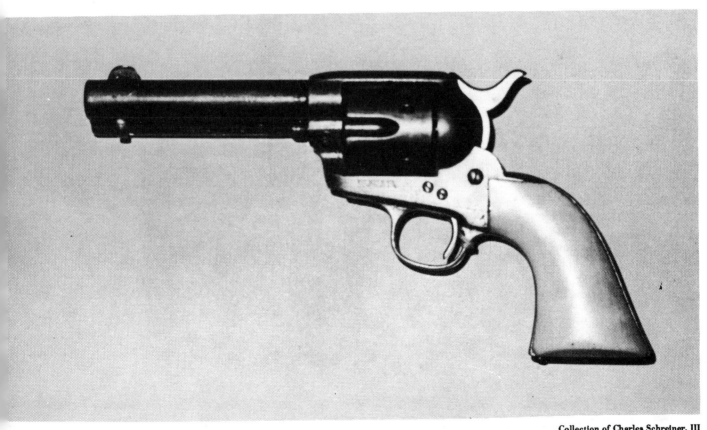

SN 283083. This .45 cal. revolver manufactured in 1906 was carried by Texas Ranger Billy J. Gunn, Company F. He served under Capatin Clint Peoples and his Ranger service was from April 1, 1966, to Sept. 1, 1986.

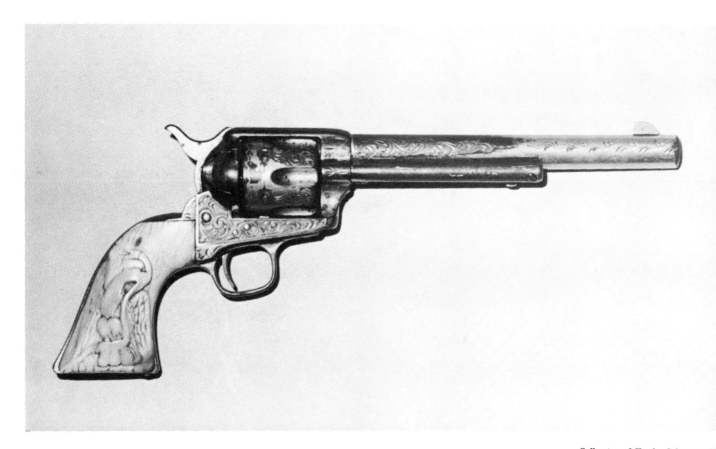

SN 501. This .44 cal. rimfire, 7 1/2" bbl., factory engraved with carved eagle & snake ivory grips belonged to Lt. Francisco Caballero, Mexican Customs Agent.

Collection of Charles Schreiner, II

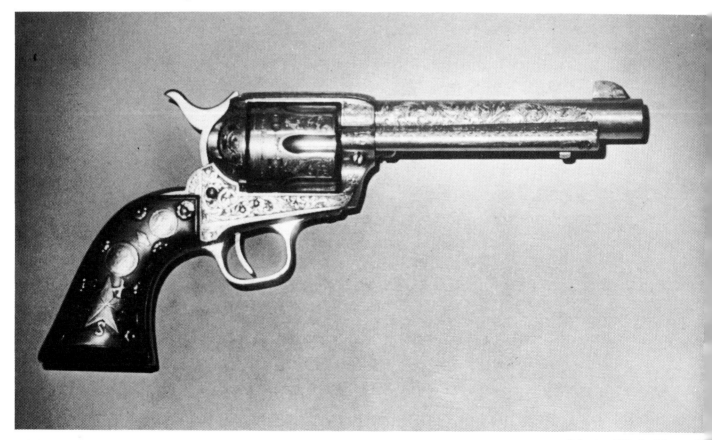

SN 336022. This .45 cal., 5 1/2" bbl. was manufactured in 1917 and is factory engraved. This revolver has Eagle Pass, Texas history. Note the unusual Texas star (non-factory) in grip.

Collection of Charles Schreiner, II

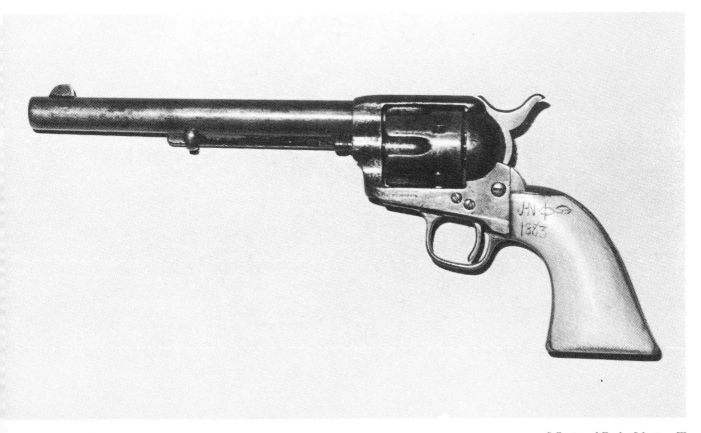

Collection of Charles Schreiner, III

N 816. This .44 cal., Rimfire was the personal sidearm of J. H. Newberry, Deputy Sheriff, Live Oak County, Texas. Note the ne-piece ivory grip with markings. The "JHN" is Mr. Newberry's cattle brand, along with his cattle ear-mark, and the 1883 ate make these very interesting grips.

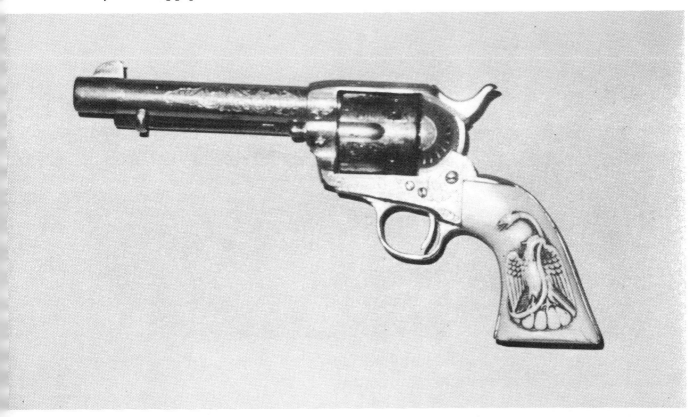

Collection of Charles Schreiner, III

N 332845. This .45 cal., 5 1/2" bbl., engraved revolver, manufactured in 1916 belonged to Texas Ranger Captain William N. anson, Uvalde County, in the early 1920s. Note Mexican eagle & snake carved ivory grips.

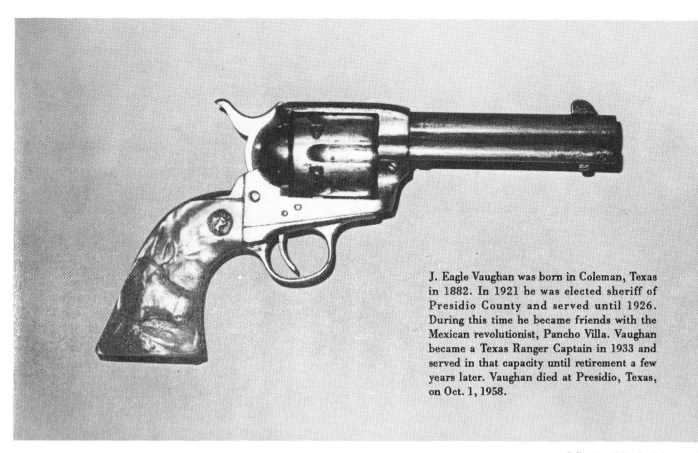

J. Eagle Vaughan was born in Coleman, Texas in 1882. In 1921 he was elected sheriff of Presidio County and served until 1926. During this time he became friends with the Mexican revolutionist, Pancho Villa. Vaughan became a Texas Ranger Captain in 1933 and served in that capacity until retirement a few years later. Vaughan died at Presidio, Texas, on Oct. 1, 1958.

Collection of Charles Schreiner,

SN 330576. This .45 cal., 4 3/4" bbl., long flute revolver was manufactured in 1915 and used by Texas Ranger J. Eagle Vaughan

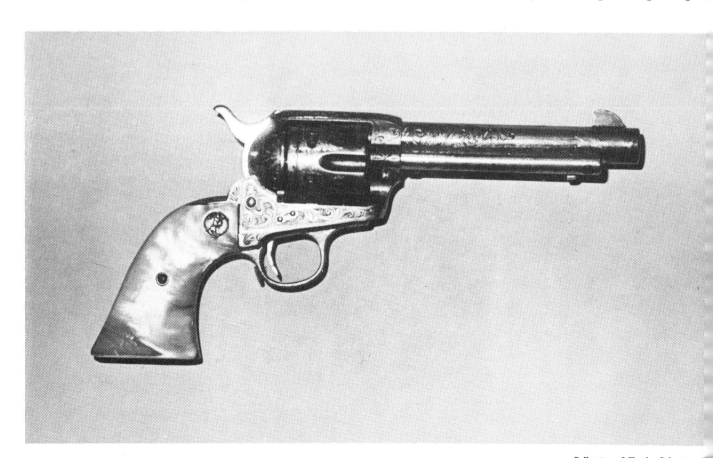

Collection of Charles Schreiner,

SN 324489. This B engraved revolver with 5 1/2" bbl. was used by J. P. Freeman, U.S. Inspector 1931-1934.

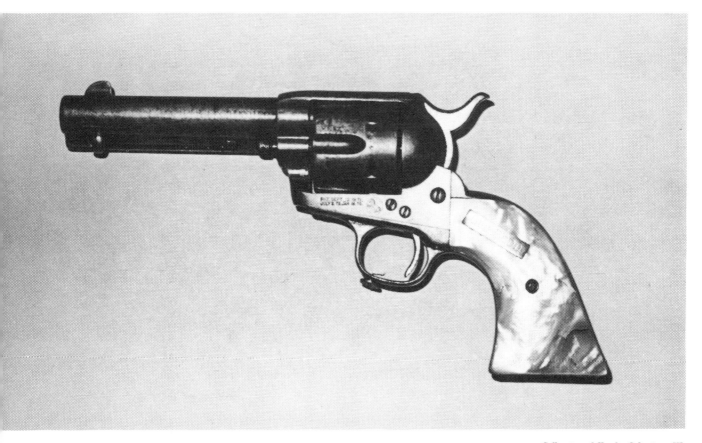

Collection of Charles Schreiner, III

N 143124. This .45 cal., 4 3/4" bbl. with carved pearl grips was manufactured in 1891 and belonged to Texas Ranger George Dodd. Note name in grip. The right grip is adorned with a carved steerhead.

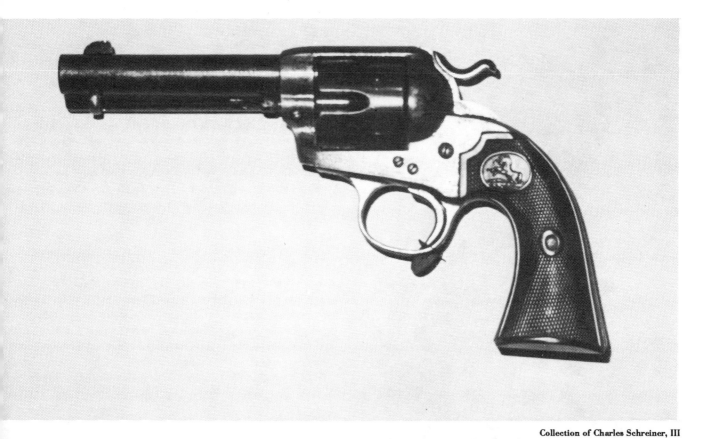

Collection of Charles Schreiner, III

N 203250. This .45 cal., 4 3/4" bbl., blue finish, Bisley model was manufactured in 1901 and shipped to Charles H. Hummel San Antonio, Texas. It belonged to "Uncle Billy" Whorton.

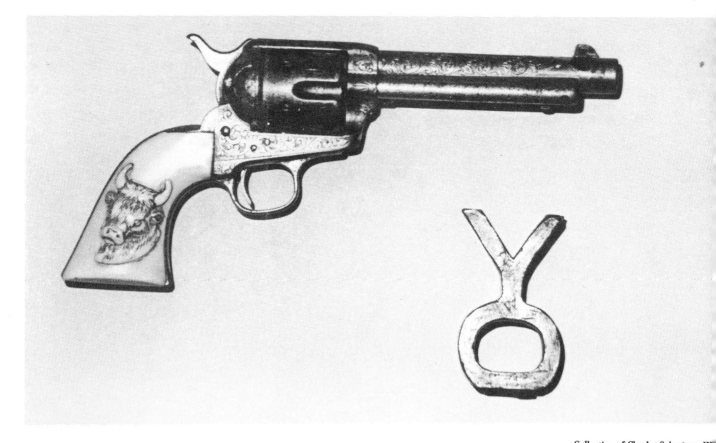

Collection of Charles Schreiner, III

SN 128145. This .45 cal., 5 1/2" bbl., nickel finish, manufactured in 1889, factory engraved revolver was owned by Black Jack Ketchum.

Black Jack Ketchum

Thomas E. Ketchum, alias "Black Jack," was a native of Texas, and was raised in the Knickerbocker community, between San Angelo and Sherwood. He was a cowboy and cattle worker, and was employed in the late 1880s and early 1890s by the big outfits of the Pecos river country and in New Mexico. Nearly six feet tall, with black hair and piercing eyes of the same hue, regular features and erect of figure, weighing perhaps 180 pounds, he was a picture of well developed manhood. He turned outlaw in about 1892, and for some ten years he and his organized associates operated successfully in Texas, Arizona, New Mexico and Colorado. Some of the members of his gang were his brother, Sam Ketchum, Will McGuinnes, Will Carver, Cole Young, and Bronco Bill, and during this time they were responsible for more than half the daring robberies in the states mentioned, murdering more people, it was said, than all other lawless gangs that ever, in organized array, infested that territory. "Black Jack" Ketchum was hanged at Clayton, New Mexico, April 26, 1901. By a strange fate Ketchum was never tried for any of the murders laid to his charge, but was hanged for 'assault upon a railway train, with intent to commit felony," which at the time of his indictment carried with it the death penalty in New Mexico.

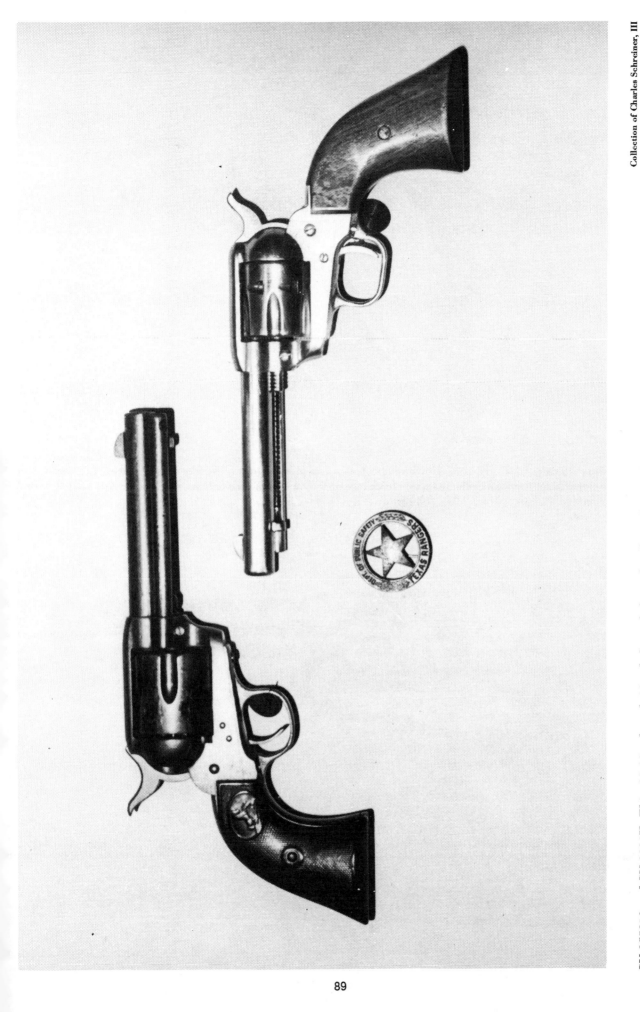

SN 255819 and SN 9922K. This .32-20 cal. and .22 cal. Scout belonged to Texas Ranger Captain A. Y. Allee. Alfred Y. Allee, Sr. was captain of Co. D located in Carrizo Springs, Texas. Captain Allee was one of the rangers primarily responsible for keeping law and order in the lower Rio Grande Valley during the 1967 labor disputes. Four generations of Allees have been Rangers beginning with Alfred's grandfather.

Collection of Charles Schreiner, III

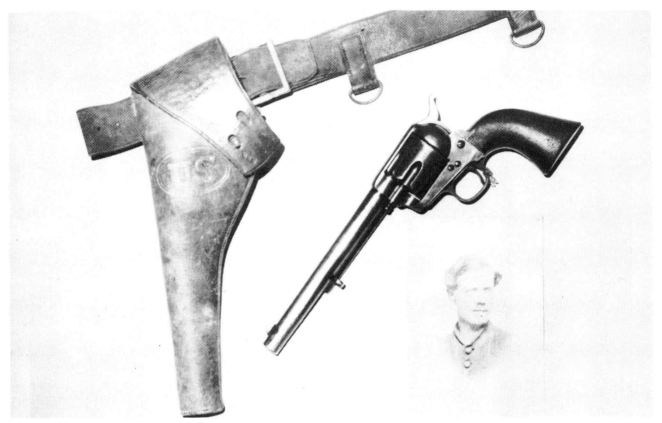

Collection of Charles Schreiner, III

SN 82885. This .45 cal., 7 1/2" bbl., blue finish revolver with one-piece walnut grips was manufactured in 1882. It was owned by General John Lapham Bullis, who was in charge of the American forces during the last Indian raid in Texas around Ingram and Mountain Home. Camp Bullis was named in his honor.

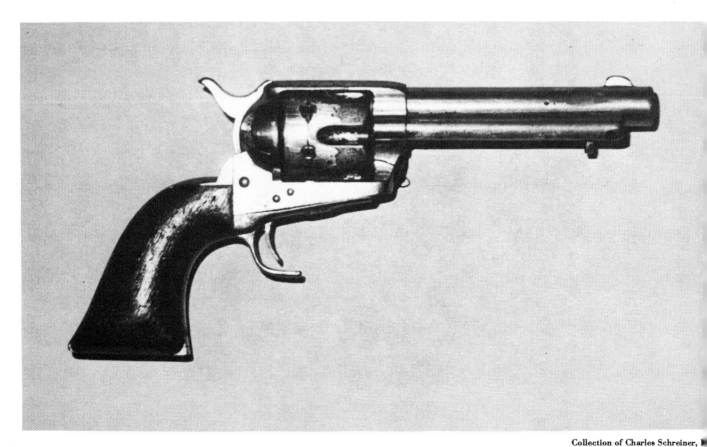

Collection of Charles Schreiner, III

SN 18222. This .45 cal. revolver with a cut-a-way triggerguard is pictured in the Times-Life Series, The Gunfighters, page 44.

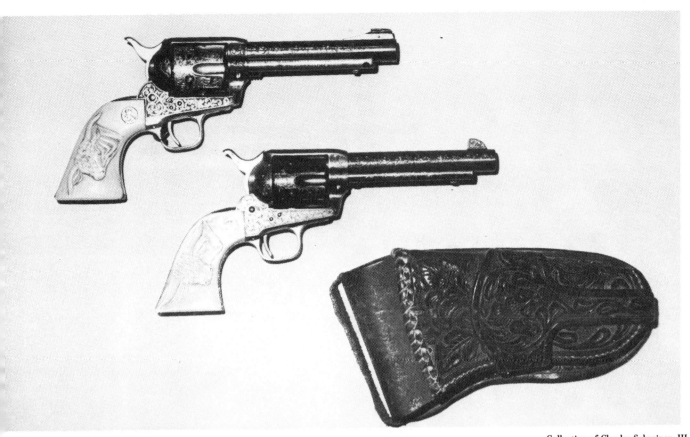

SN 352307 (upper) and SN 342234. These .45 cal., 5 1/2" bbl., nickel finish, engraved revolvers were used by Texas Ranger Captain William W. Sterling. "Texas Ranger Captain W. W. Sterling" is factory gold inlayed on the backstrap.

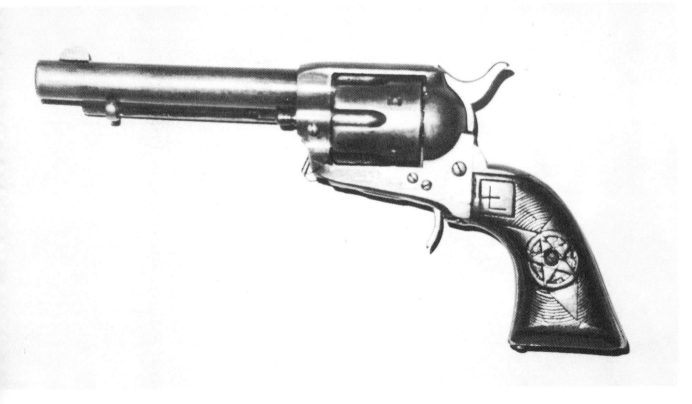

SN 248657. This revolver was also owned by Texas Ranger Captain W. W. Sterling. Sterling is the author of *Trails and Trials of a Texas Ranger*. Note the unusual grips and the removal of the trigger guard. This was done because of Captain Sterling's unusually large hands. This revolver was manufactured in 1903.

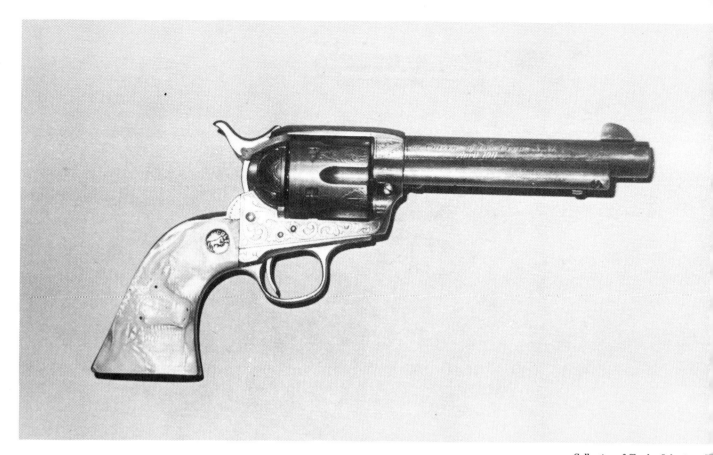

SN 317839. This .45 cal., 5 1/2" bbl. revolver manufactured in 1911 was presented to A. A. Sena, by Citizens of Las Vegas, New Mexico and is so-inscribed on the barrel. Note the nice carved pearl steerhead grips with recessed medallions.

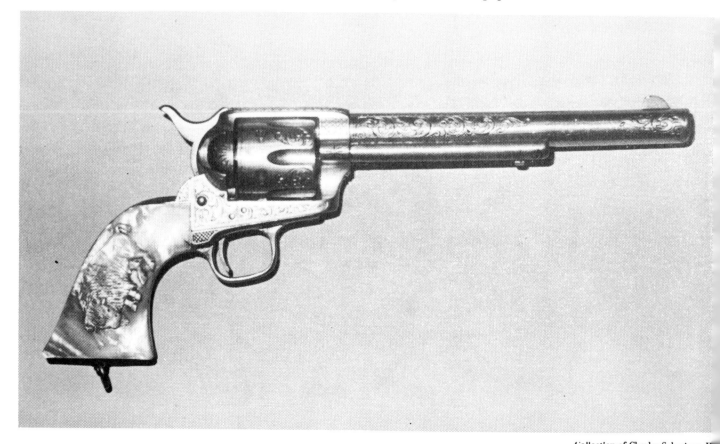

SN 24844. This .45 cal., 7 1/2" bbl. was shipped in 1876 to Schuyler, Hartley, and Graham, New York City, N.Y. Note the beautiful carved pearl buffalo on grip. It is factory engraved and has a lanyard ring in butt.

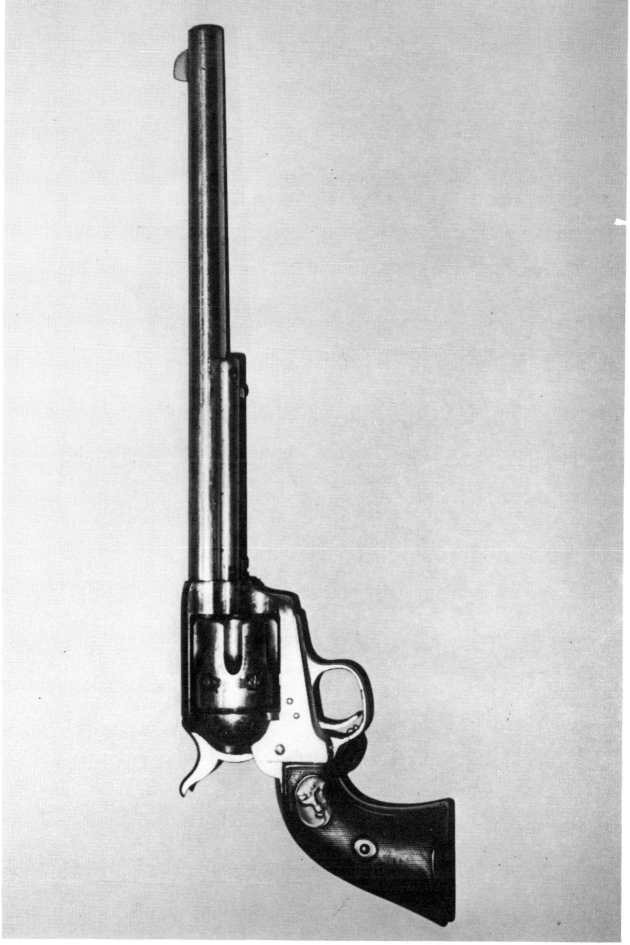

SN 147247. According to Colt ledgers this Colt .45, 10 1/2" bbl., left the factory in 1892 for Colt's agency in San Francisco, California.

Collection of Charles Schreiner, III

"OLD LUCKY"

SN 314012. This .45 cal., 4 3/4" bbl., factory engraved revolver was the favorite of Texas Ranger Frank Hamer. He affectionately named this Colt "Old Lucky." This is one of the most well-known revolvers to be photographed for this book.

Collection of Charles Schreiner, III

Frank Hamer
1884 - 1955

Frank Hamer was born in Fairview, Texas in 1884.

He joined Captain John H. Rogers' Company C in April, 1906, and became Captain of that company in 1912. He was transferred to Austin only a few months later to command Headquarters Company. He was instrumental in the cleaning up of many oil towns and in solving the Engler Murder case, the Corpus Christi bomb case and the Leakey case. During his forty years of service in law enforcement he held many other posts, including Marshal of Navasota, special police officer for the Mayor of Houston and as an agent of the United States Prohibition Service. As a special agent for the Texas Prison System, Hamer tracked down two of the country's most notorious law-breakers—Clyde Barrow and Bonnie Parker. The two were slain in a spectacular shootout on May 23, 1934.

Hamer died in Austin, Texas, on July 10, 1955.

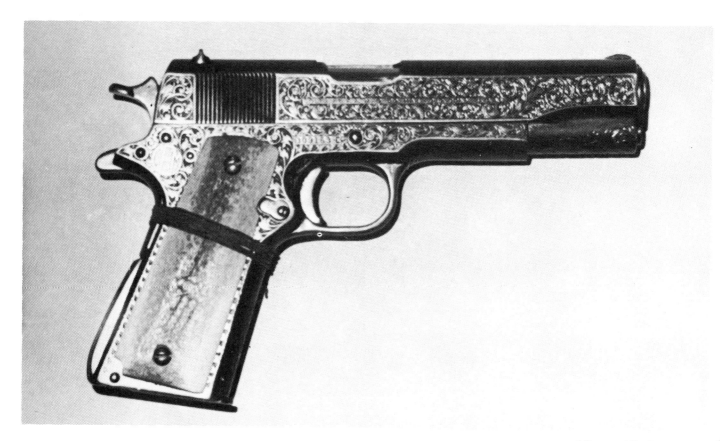

SN 309163. This 45 cal. automatic was the sidearm of Texas Ranger Charlie Miller. Note the monogram on grip.

Collection of Charles Schreiner, III

RANGER CHARLIE MILLER

Charlie Miller started his remarkable career as a deputy sheriff in Bexar County, then joined the Rangers in 1919, at Del Rio, Texas, under Captain W. W. Davis, Company E. Over the ensuing fifty years he served under several of the most effective Captains and participated in a number of celebrated enforcement episodes. He commanded the respect of everyone, including his commanders, and was honored with a special party at the Y-O Ranch near Kerrville when he was retired in 1968.

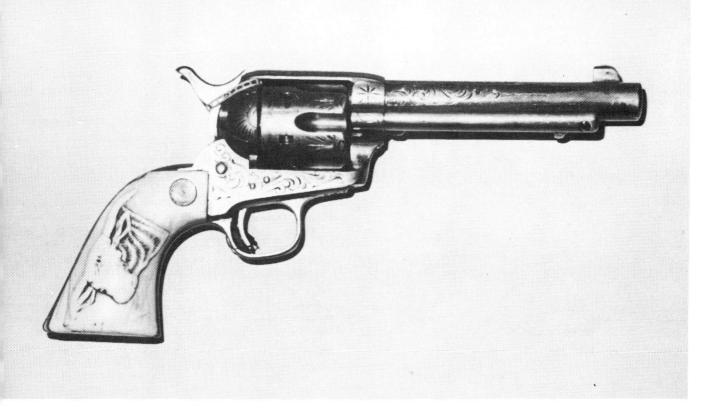

Collection of Charles Schreiner, III

114669. This .45 cal., 5 1/2" bbl., nickel finish, engraved revolver was shipped to Hartley & Graham, New York, New York, April 18, 1885. Senator George Luckey from California once owned this firearm.

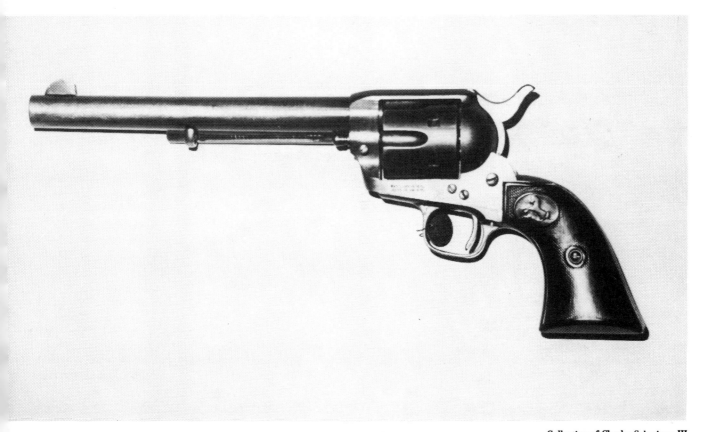

Collection of Charles Schreiner, III

353046. This .45 cal., 7 1/2" bbl., blue finish revolver was shipped February 27, 1929, to the 101 Ranch, Ponca City, Oklahoma. There were fifteen guns in this shipment.

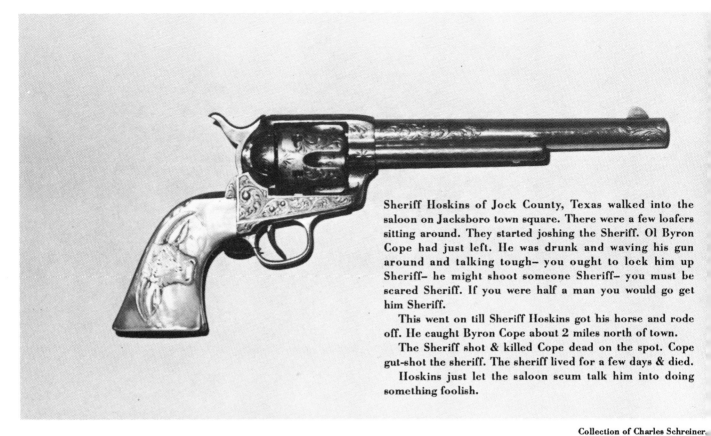

Sheriff Hoskins of Jock County, Texas walked into the saloon on Jacksboro town square. There were a few loafers sitting around. They started joshing the Sheriff. Ol Byron Cope had just left. He was drunk and waving his gun around and talking tough— you ought to lock him up Sheriff— he might shoot someone Sheriff— you must be scared Sheriff. If you were half a man you would go get him Sheriff.

This went on till Sheriff Hoskins got his horse and rode off. He caught Byron Cope about 2 miles north of town.

The Sheriff shot & killed Cope dead on the spot. Cope gut-shot the sheriff. The sheriff lived for a few days & died.

Hoskins just let the saloon scum talk him into doing something foolish.

Collection of Charles Schreiner

SN 111059. This .45 cal., 7 1/2" bbl., factory engraved revolver was the personal sidearm of H.M. Hoskins, Sheriff of Ja County, Texas. Hoskins shot Byron Cope with this revolver.

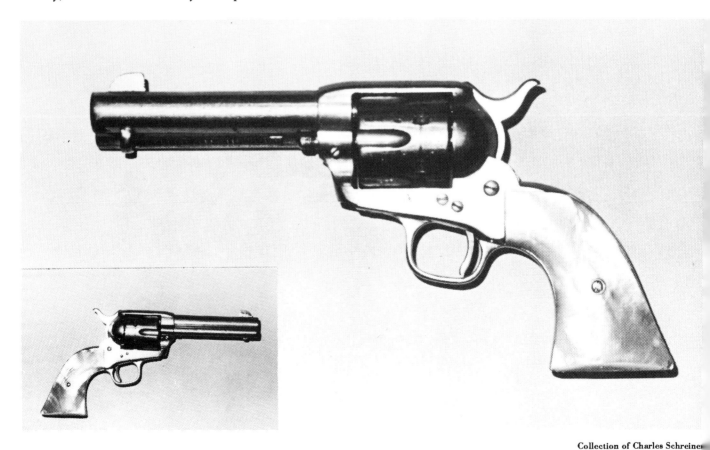

Collection of Charles Schreiner

SN 337288. According to the Factory letter this .45 cal., 4 3/4" bbl., nickel finish revolver with pearl grips was shipped F 15, 1919, to the State of Texas, Austin Texas. Shipment of one. Reckon who got this one?

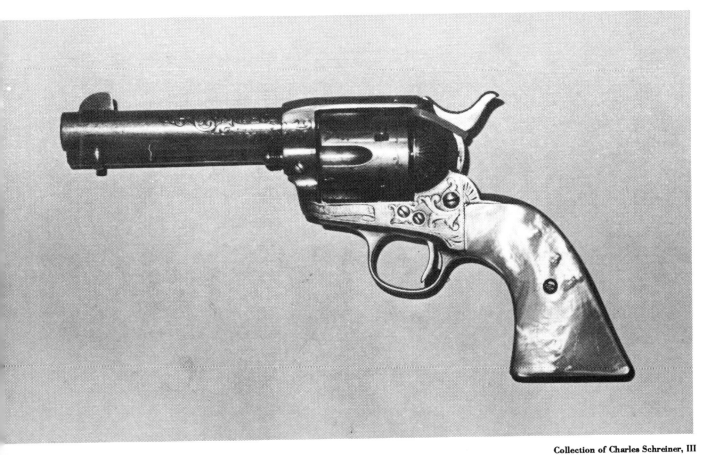

Collection of Charles Schreiner, III

N 324908. This .45 cal., 4 3/4" bbl. engraved revolver was manufactured in 1912 and was the sidearm of Texas Ranger Crosby Marsden. It is engraved and silver finished.

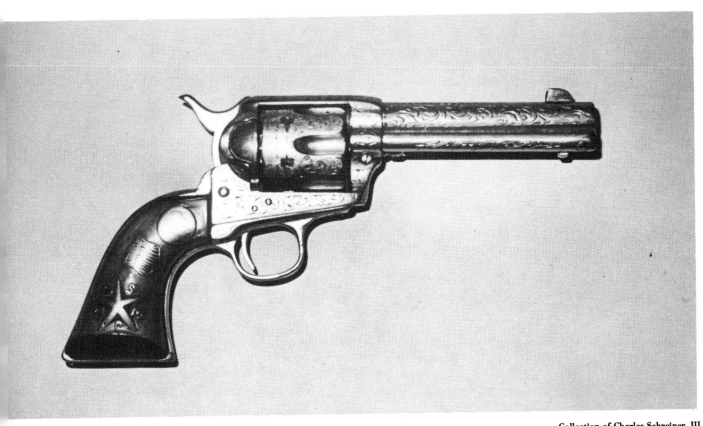

Collection of Charles Schreiner, III

N 181718 This .45 cal., 4 3/4" bbl. was manufactured in 1898 and used by Texas Ranger Jesse Perez, Rio Grande City. Perez served under Captain John Hughes.

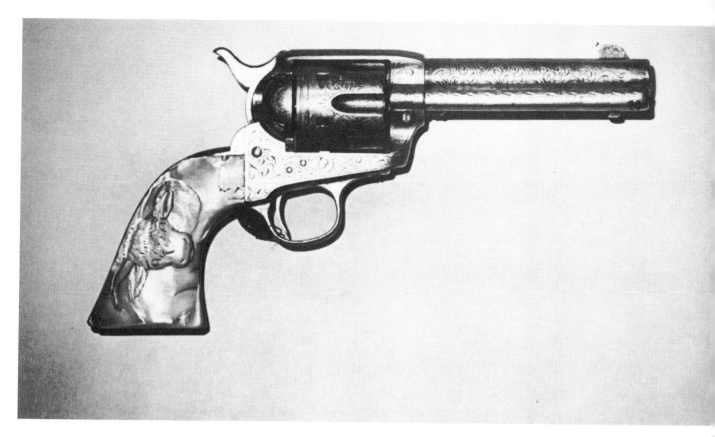

SN 309834. This .45 cal., 4 3/4" bbl., factory engraved revolver with carved steerhead pearl grips was used by Sheriff W. H Flynn, Lubbock, Texas. Colt shipped the gun directly to him according to factory records.

Collection of Charles Schreiner, II

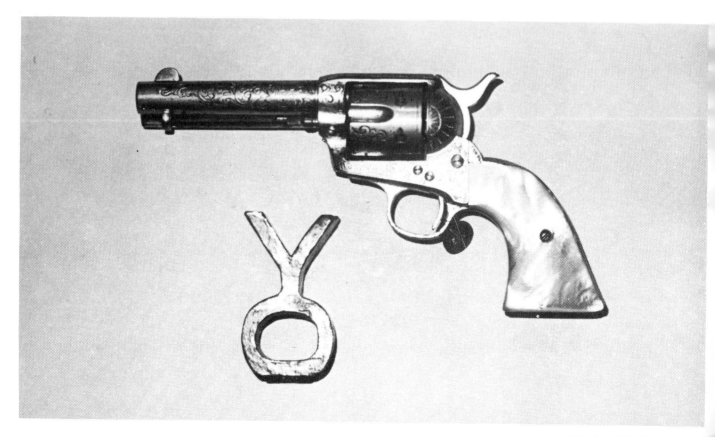

SN 266027. This .45 cal., 4 3/4" bbl., factory engraved Colt was manufactured in 1905 and was the sidearm of Texas Ranger Captain W. W. Taylor.

Collection of Charles Schreiner, III

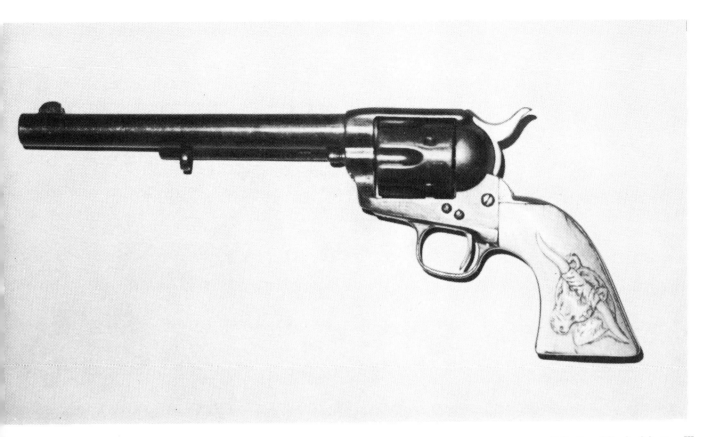

Collection of Charles Schreiner, III

N 39995. This .45 cal., 7 1/2" bbl., revolver with carved ivory steerhead on left side was manufactured in 1877. This firearm marked R✠M on top of backstrap. This means "Republica Mexicana."

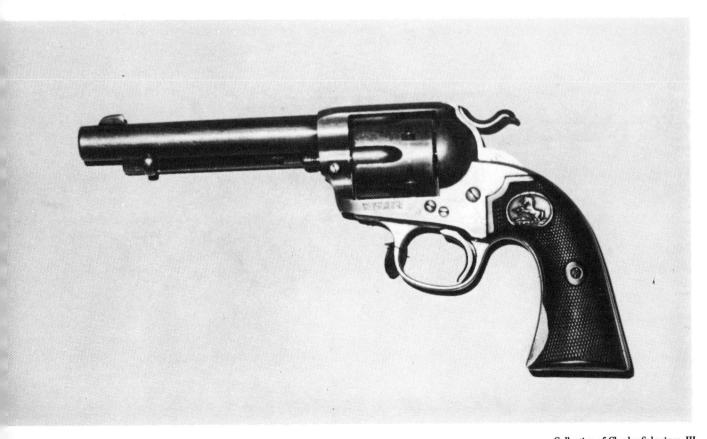

Collection of Charles Schreiner, III

N 248574. This .45 cal., 5 1/2" bbl., Bisley revolver was shipped to the famous Copper Queen Mining Company in Bisbee, Arizona, in 1903.

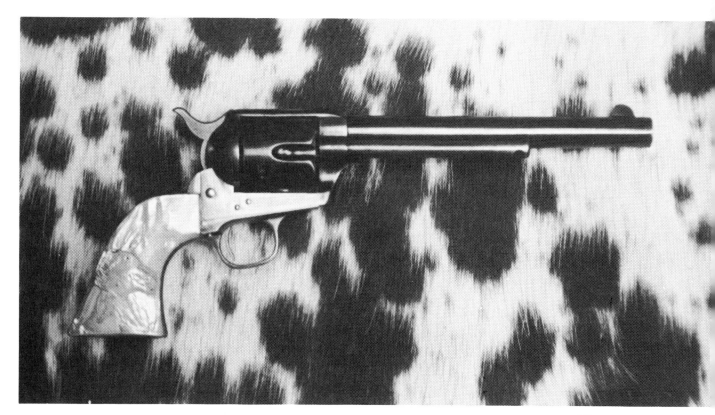

Collection of Charles Schreiner, I

SN 95118. This .44-40 cal., 7 1/2" bbl., blue finish Frontier Six-Shooter with carved steerhead pearl grips was manufacture in 1883. Inscribed on the backstrap is "J.X. Biedler, Miles City, 1883." Biedler was a famous western marshal. He wa credited with cleaning up the Montana road agents. Biedler died in Helena, Montana.

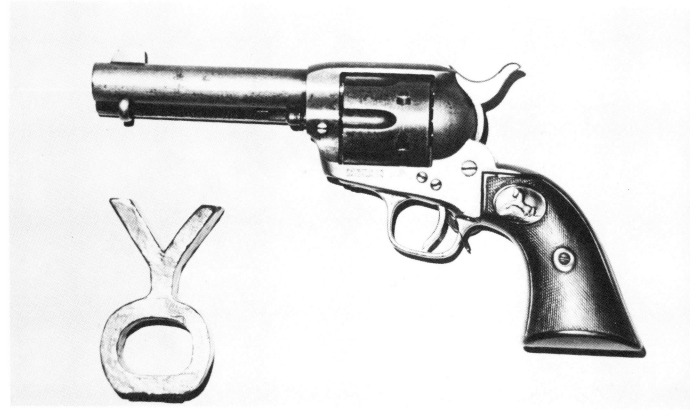

Collection of Charles Schreiner, I

SN 338432. This .38-40 cal., 4 3/4" bbl. revolver was manufactured in 1920. "Uncle Billy" Clegg, breeder of American Quarte Horse Association's #1 walking horse, "Wimpy". Clegg was affiliated with the famous King Ranch in South Texas.

Collection of Charles Schreiner, III

SN YO 75. This .45 cal., 7 1/2" bbl., revolver was produced in 1980 especially for the YO Ranch in Texas. Note the ivory grips with YO markings. The engraving was done by Frank Hendricks. Only 200 were produced commemorating the 100th anniversary of the famous YO Ranch.

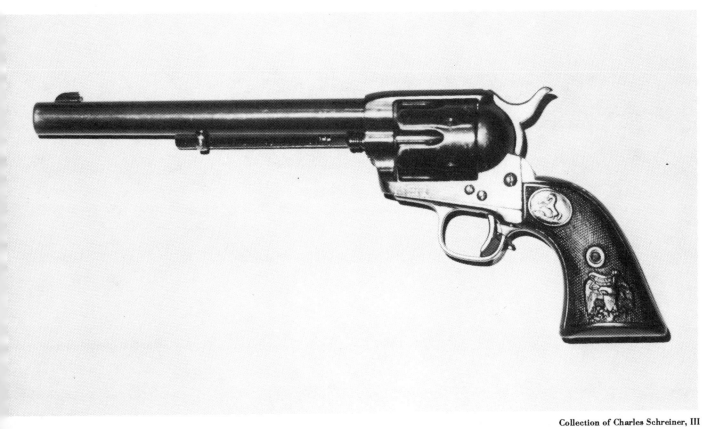

Collection of Charles Schreiner, III

SN 1862. This is a .22 cal., 7 1/2" bbl. revolver manufactured during the black powder range. Only 107 revolvers were produced in .22 caliber.

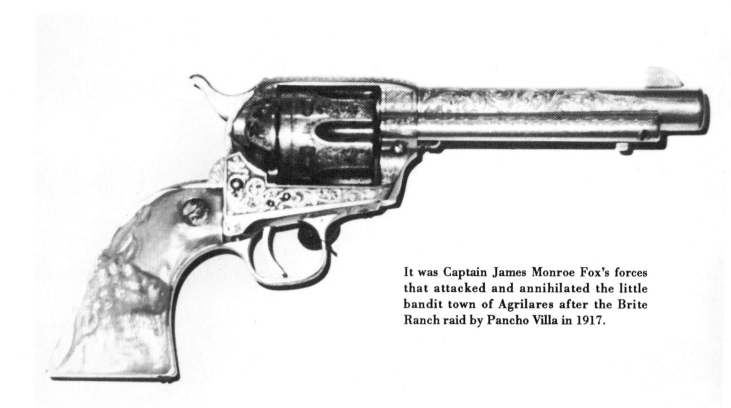

It was Captain James Monroe Fox's forces that attacked and annihilated the little bandit town of Agrilares after the Brite Ranch raid by Pancho Villa in 1917.

Collection of Charles Schreiner, III

SN 335030. This .45 cal., factory engraved, 5 1/2" bbl. was the sidearm of Texas Ranger Captain James Monroe Fox. Note the fine carved steerhead pearl stocks with recessed Colt medallions (facing forward). This Colt was manufactured in 1917.

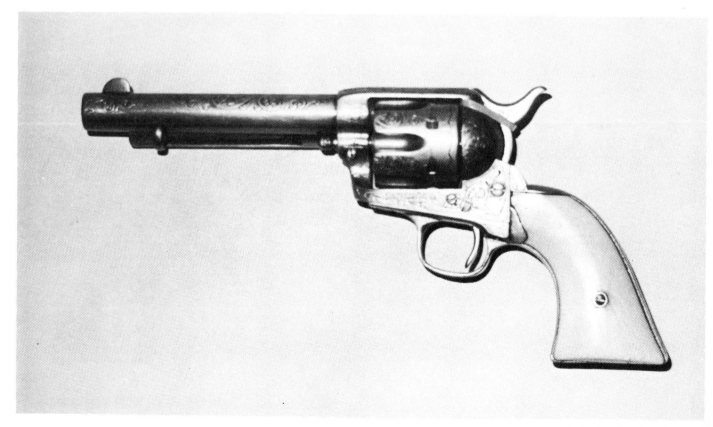

Collection of Charles Schreiner, III

SN 166511. This .45 cal., 5 1/2" bbl., factory engraved revolver with 2-piece ivory stocks was shipped June 3, 1896, directly to Lt. John J. Brooks, Arizona Rangers, Hagters, Tucson, Arizona. One in shipment. This firearm was silver plated before leaving the Colt factory.

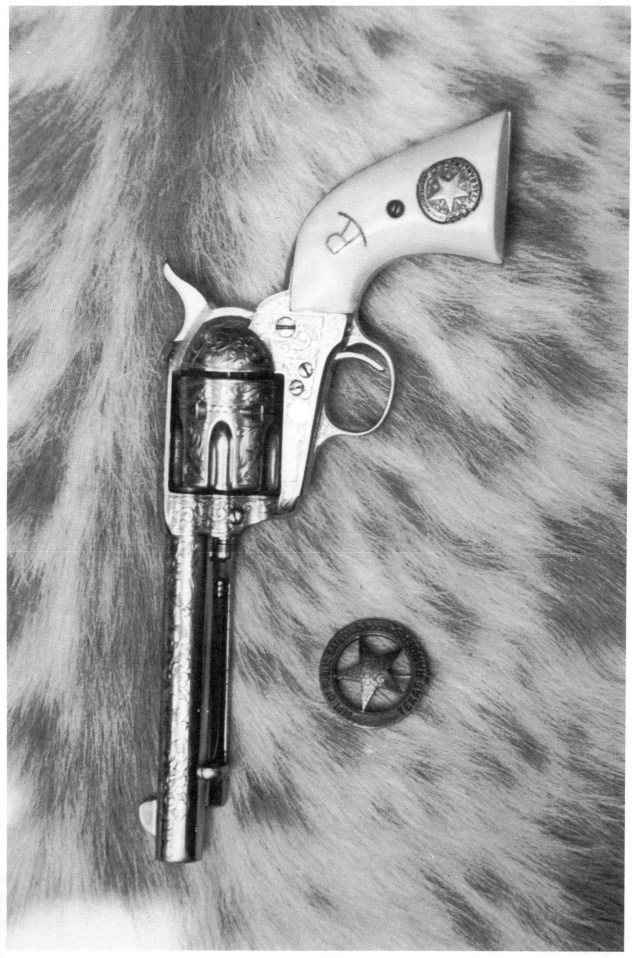

SN 231513. This .45 cal., 5 1/2" bbl., nickel finish revolver manufactured in 1892 is factory engraved and was used by Texas Ranger Walter Russell. During the early 1920s Russell served as an Arizona Ranger. He later served as Texas Ranger with Company D in Alice, Texas. Russell retired in 1967. Note the "R" and Texas Ranger badge in left ivory grip.

Collection of Charles Schreiner, III

Collection of Charles Schreiner, III

SN 81843. This .45 cal., 7 1/2" bbl., blue finish revolver was the sidearm of Texas Ranger James Cawthorn. Note the gold-inlaid Texas long-horn steer in the barrel, and the nice engraving. The pearl grips add to the beauty of this fine piece.

Collection of Charles Schreiner

SN 53291. This .45 cal., 4 3/4" bbl., revolver was manufactured in 1880. and was used in a shooting incident in Kerrvi Texas on March 23, 1939.

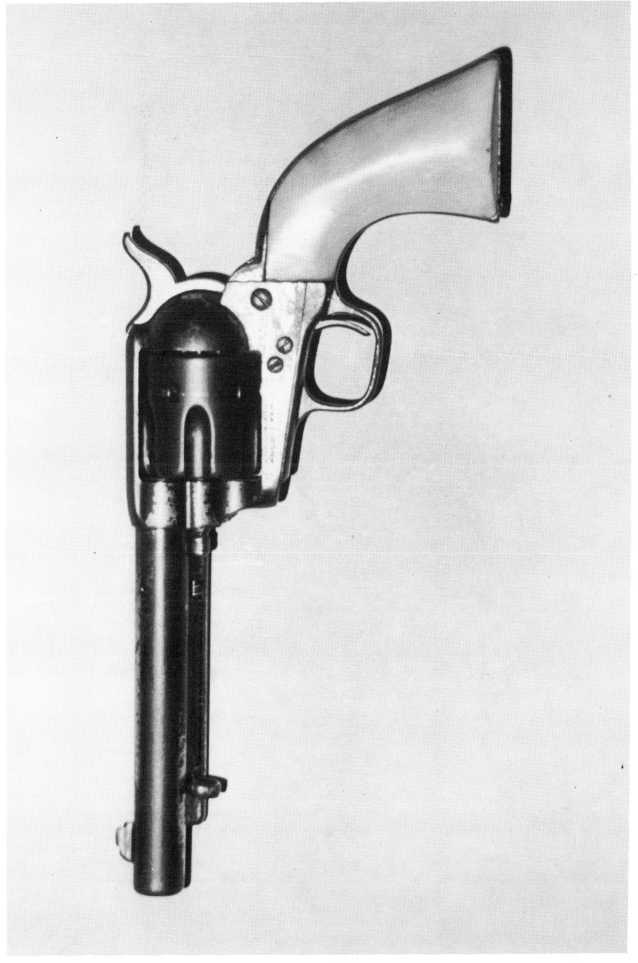

Serial #2! This is the second Colt single-action to be produced. The 45 cal., 7 1/2" bbl., manufactured in 1873, was not shipped until 5 years later to Degress in Mexico. The barrel has been shortened and the one-piece ivory grips are not original.

Collection of Charles Schreiner, III

On the far right in the cowgirl photo is Ruth Roach, one of the famous early cowgirls. Back in the early days, women competed head to head with men in many events they are no longer allowed to participate in, including Bronco riding ! The equality came to an end when several women were seriously injured and killed in the more dangerous events. Needless to say N.O.W. was not there at that time to ensure their right to a premature death under a falling bronco.

The upper photo shows a number of items of Ruth's, resting on a original 101 Ranch trunk, including her chaps, gauntlets and a Colt New Service revolver in 44-40 caliber with her name engraved on the backstrap. Contrary to popular myth, many western men and women preferred the more modern double action revolvers to the old Colt Single Action as it was faster into action and could be carried safely with six rounds in the cylinder. The 44-40 round was interchangeable in the 1892 Winchester lever action rifle/carbine. 44-40 cartridges were also available loaded with fine bird shot which made trick shooting easier and less likely to cause casualties in the crowd of spectators.

A group of souvenir postcards from the famous 101 Ranch in Bliss, Oklahoma. The upper two are views of Bill Pickett, the famous black cowboy who pioneered the rodeo sport of Steer Wrestling.

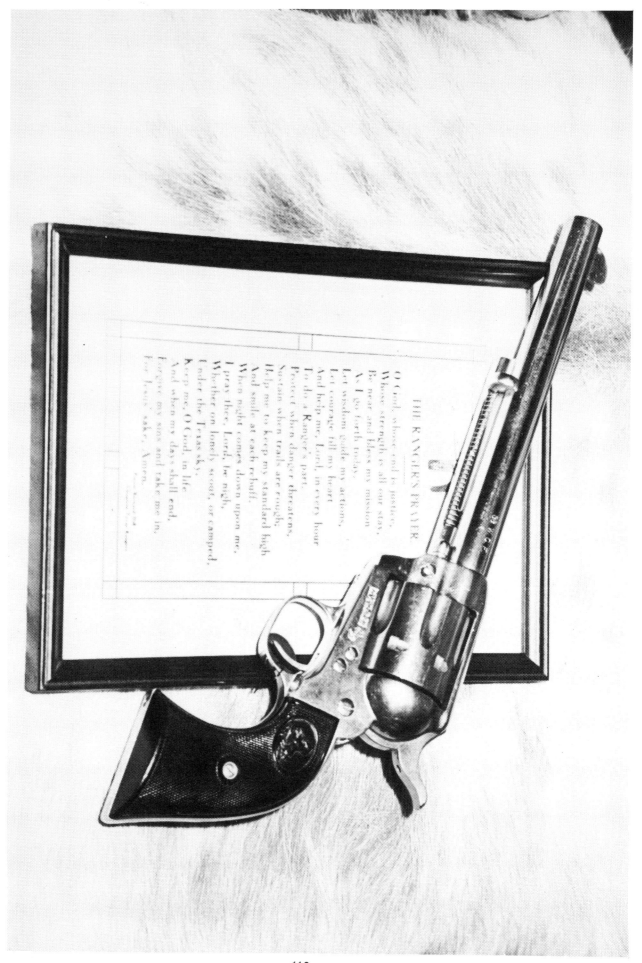

SN 349215. This .38-40 cal., 7 1/2" bbl., nickel finish revolver was the personal sidearm of Texas Ranger Captain Pierre B. Hill. He also served as chaplain of the Rangers and wrote "*A Ranger's Prayer.*" He also authored a book, "*For God and Texas.*" This Colt revolver is in near-mint condition, and was manufactured in 1927.

Collection of Charles Schreiner, III

At the right of the page is a Marlin pump model 42, 12 gauge shotgun in almost new condition. It is engraved on the left side of the receiver, commemorating a famous rodeo site and a friendship between two of America's early premier cowgirls. The inscriptions read; "Triangle R Ranch" and below that " To Mabel Strickland from her friend Fox Hastings".

Mabel is shown above on the left and Fox on the right.

Collection of Paul Sorrel

SN 86922. This .44-40 cal., 7 1/2" bbl., nickel finish with beautiful carved Mexican Eagle and Snake ivory grips was factory engraved and shipped July 17, 1883, to Wexell & Degress, Mexico City, Mexico. Shipment of 4.

Collection of Paul Sorrel

SN 86922. Right side frame view showing intricate engraving pattern. It is believed this firearm was in the collection of Porfirio Diaz, President of Mexico.

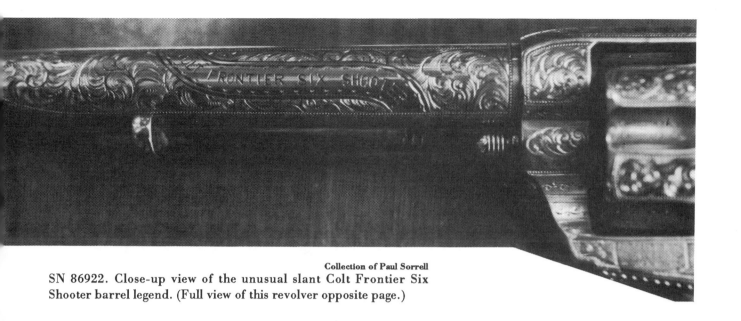

SN 86922. Close-up view of the unusual slant Colt Frontier Six Shooter barrel legend. (Full view of this revolver opposite page.)

Collection of Paul Sorrell

Porfirio Diaz was known to be an avid gun collector. He entered the army and served with distinction in three different wars: the War with the United States (1846-48); the Civil War (1857-60); and the Patriotic War (1863-67) against the attempt of Emperor Napoleon III of France to make Mexico a French dependency. Diaz was an outstanding Mexican general in that war. He overthrew the government of President Sebastian Lerdo de Tejada in 1876 and was installed as President the following year. He remained in power until 1911. It is believed he owned the beautiful Colt Frontier Six-Shooter Serial # 86922.

PORFIRIO DIAZ
President of Mexico
1830 - 1915

Collection of Paul Sorre[llo]

SN 331270. This .45 cal., 4 3/4" bbl., silver finish factory engraved revolver was shipped on January 20, 1915, to C. L. Bering Jr., Houston, Texas, with Pearl carved steerhead grips. Note the long-flute cylinder. This was the personal sidearm of Din[g] Hagen, Sheriff of Fort Bend County, Texas from 1915 to 1918 and from 1923 to 1926.

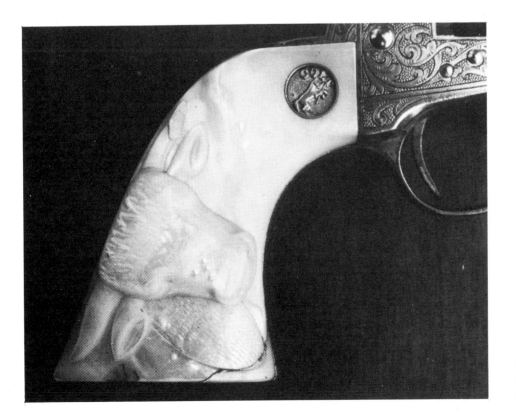

Collection of Paul Sorr[ello]

SN 331270. Close-up view of Factor[y] carved pearl steerhead grips wit[h] Colt medallion.

Collection of Paul Sorrell

SN 258488. This .45 cal., 3 1/2" bbl., blue finish Sheriff's Model left the Colt Factory Sept. 20, 1904, bound for Walter Tips Co. c/o John R. Parker, Austin, Texas. Shipment of one.

Collection of Paul Sorrell

SN 162338. Factory records state this .45 cal., 4" bbl., blue finish. Sheriff's Model was shipped April 27, 1896, to J. S. Dunlay Hdwe., Houston Texas. The gun is fitted with beautiful one-piece ivory grips.

SN 123287. No Factory information is available on this revolver. However this .45 cal., 3 1/2" bbl., Sheriff's Model is considered to be original. Colt information with this revolver states that serial # 123286 and #123288 were shipped with 3 1/2" bbls. The gun is fitted with nice one-piece ivory grips.

SN 304970. This .45 cal., 5 1/2" bbl., silver finish revolver was shipped April 1, 1908, to Schoverling, Daly, & Gales, New York, New York. Shipped with carved pearl oxhead on right grip. Documented to be the personal sidearm of Walter G. Musick, deputy sheriff in Socorro County, New Mexico. The revolver was a presentation to him from friends in that county.

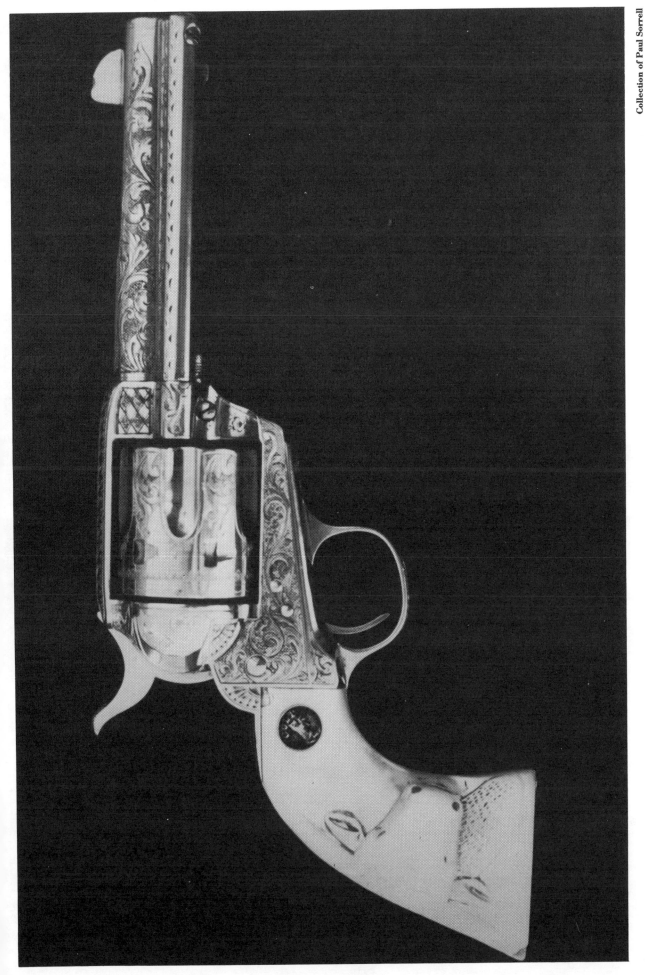

Collection of Paul Sorrell

SN 333256. This beautifully engraved .45 cal., 4 3/4" bbl. nickel revolver was shipped with pearl, carved steerhead grips to the Praeger Hardware Co., San Antonio, Texas, on August 26, 1916. Shipment of two. This was the personal sidearm of D. S. "Dud" Barker, Texas Ranger. Barker served under captain Bill McDonald at San Saba. Also was Sheriff of Peco County (Fort Stockton) 1906-1926. Barker was credited with killing twenty-two men.

SN 251875. This engraved .41 cal., 5 1/2" bbl., mfg. in 1904, was used by Floyd Randolph, Sheriff of Carter County, Oklahoma from 1935 to 1943. He also was a rodeo performer with the 101 Ranch Show, and was personal friends with Roy Rogers. No factory information is available on this revolver.

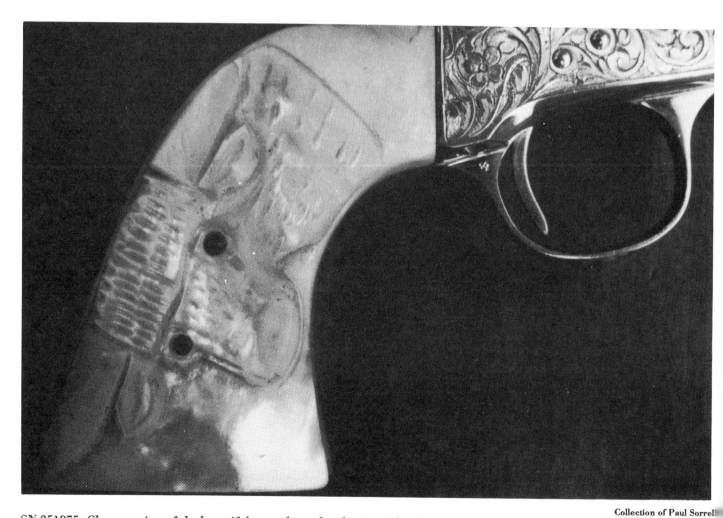

SN 251875. Close-up view of the beautiful carved steerhead grips with ruby eyes.

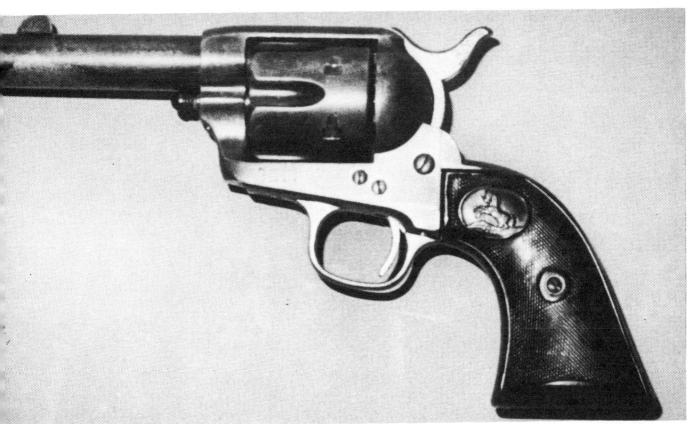

Collection of Paul Sorrell

122365. This .45 cal., 3 1/2" bbl., Sheriff's Model was shipped in 1887 to J. S. Dunlay Hardware, Houston, Texas.

Collection of Paul Sorrell

(Left) A nice single-loop, single action Sheriff's Model holster with cartouche marked W. D. BREWER, MAKER, MUSCOGEEE, OKLA. (Right) Another fine example of a single-loop holster hall-marked W. H. CLAY, BROWNSVILLE, TEXAS, for a 4 3/4" bbl. revolver.

Collection of Paul Sorre

This photo of Texas Ranger Harold Slack and his sister was taken the day Slack joined the Texas Rangers. He served with Company A in 1930's and again in 1949-50. He also served with the Border Patrol and the Secret Service.

Collection of Paul Sorrell

354056. This profusely factory engraved single action .45 cal., 4 3/4" bbl., nickel finish, ivory grips, with A. G. Lemos engraved on the backstrap was shipped to Neucis Hardware & Implement on Nov. 6, 1930. Research has documented this firearm to be the personal sidearm of Harold Slack, Texas Ranger, Co. A. from 1931 til 1933. (photos on opposite page.)

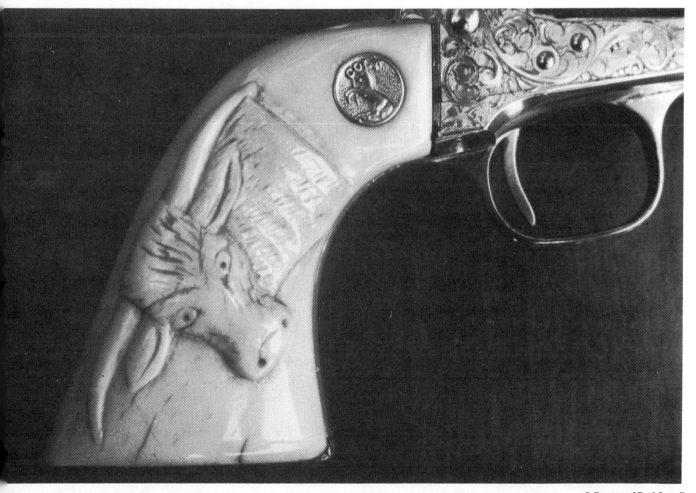

Collection of Paul Sorrell

354056. Grip view showing original carved steerhead ivory grips with Colt medallion. Note the age cracks at bottom.

SN 324096. This .38-40 cal., 4 3/4" bbl., Helfricht scroll and border engraved was shipped June, 1912, to Praeger Hardware Co., San Antonio, Texas. This is a prime example of Helfricht engraving. Note unusual pearl steerhead grip.

Collection of Paul Sorrell

Collection of Paul Sorrell

N 324096. Left side view of the Helfricht engraving. Shipped to San Antonio in 1912.

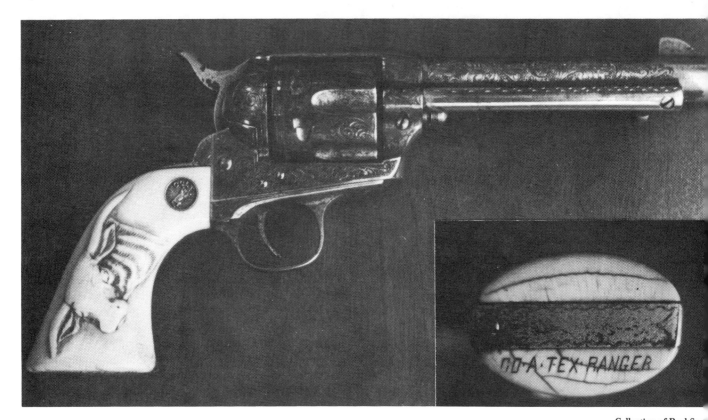

SN 333575. This factory engraved revolver .45 cal. 5 1/2" bbl., silver finish with carved ivory steerhead left the factory Dec. 1916, for Colonel J. F. Stockton, Captain J. J. Sanders, address unavailable. Shipment of one. Sanders was Captain of Co. Texas Rangers 1910-1918.

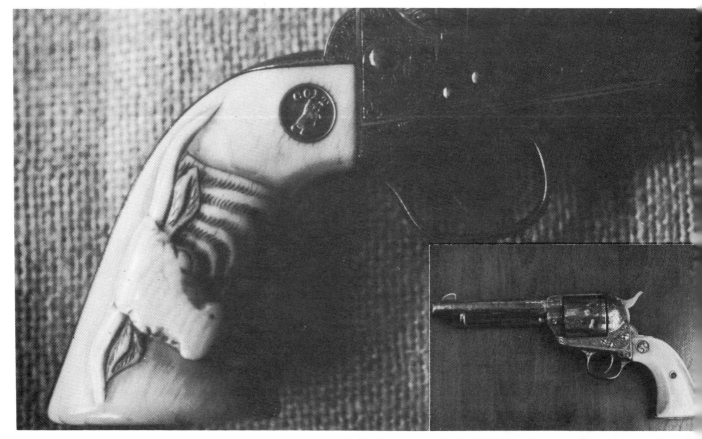

SN 333575. Grip view showing carved ivory steerhead with Colt Medallions. J. J. Sanders was sheriff of Caldwell Coun Texas 1898-1908.

Upon the trunk are three Wells Fargo & Company shotguns from the earliest days of the company through the 1900s. From the top they are; a Manton 10 gauge muzzle loading percussion gun engraved on the rib "Wells Fargo California Express", which was the original name of the company when first incorporated. Next is a 10 gauge 1887 Winchester marked "W.F.& Co." in an intertwined fashion on the opposite side of the receiver from the "WRA Co." done in the same style. Last is an 1897 Winchester solid frame pump marked "Property of Wells Fargo & Co. 12" on the left side of the receiver.

Three more old Well Fargo guns are featured here. From the top they are; a Charles Daly 10 gauge double bbl, 30" bbls, serial #193 , a Manton 10 gauge side lever double, serial #7241 and a Wm. Moore & Co. 12 gauge double serial #5836. All are marked in the metal as the property of Wells Fargo & Co.

SN 105826, .45 cal., 4 3/4" bbl, nickel finish. Shipped to Simmons Hardware Co., St. Louis, Mo., Feb. 12, 1884. Documented to belong to Sheriff D. B. (Uncle Dan) Hooks and used to kill Robert P. (Bob) Linch while attempting to make an arrest at Brandon, Texas, March 29, 1899. Said Robert P. Linch is buried in the Brandon Cemetery, Brandon, Texas.

Collection of John W. Stewart

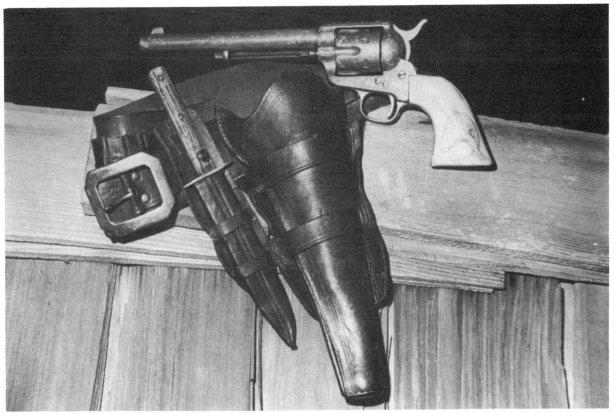

Collection of John W. Stewart

Colt, SN 75163, cal. .44/40, etch panel, 7 1/2" bbl. Shipped to Hartley & Graham for engraving Dec. 31, 1882. Close up view shows unusual steer head ivory grips. Holster rig marked Montgomery Ward with a Green River Bowie Knife.

Collection of John W. Stewart

Colt, SN 104429, cal. .44/40, etch panel, 7 1/2" bbl. Shipped with blue finish and wood grips to J. F. Schmeller & Sons, Kansas City, Kansas, Jan. 26, 1886. Shown with holster rig marked S. C. Gallup, Pueblo, Colorado.

Collection of John W. Stewart

Colt, SN 114194, .45 cal., 4 3/4" bbl, factory engraved, nickel finish, and shipped with factory carved ox head ivory stocks to E. A. Worden, Dallas, Texas, Nov. 22, 1886. Holster and money belt rig marked A. Aurbish, Rosenburg, Texas.

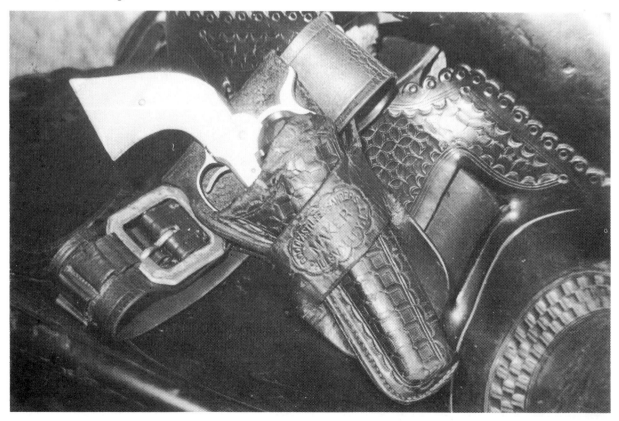

Collection of John W. Stewart

Colt, SN 231219, .38-40 cal., 4 3/4" bbl., blue finish. Shipped to Turner Hardware Co., Muskogee, (Indian Territory) Oklahoma, Aug. 21, 1902. Holster marked Goodpasture & Sanders, Pauls Valley, Indian Territory.

SN 105747. Colt .45 cal., 5 1/2" bbl, factory engraved with nickel finish. Shipped to Hartley & Graham, New York, N. Y., Aug. 21, 1884. Holster rig marked A. L. Furstnow, Miles City, Montana and saddle marked Miles City Saddlery Co., Miles City, Montana. Collection of John W. Stewart

Collection of John W. Stewart

Bisley model SN 327683, .45 cal., 5 1/2" bbl., blue finish, and shipped with carved ox head ivory stocks to Abercrombie & Fitch Co., New York, N.Y., Nov. 13, 1913. Colt shipped in shipment of one with long flute cylinder. Holster rig by Eldred & Morrow, Cheyenne, Wyoming.

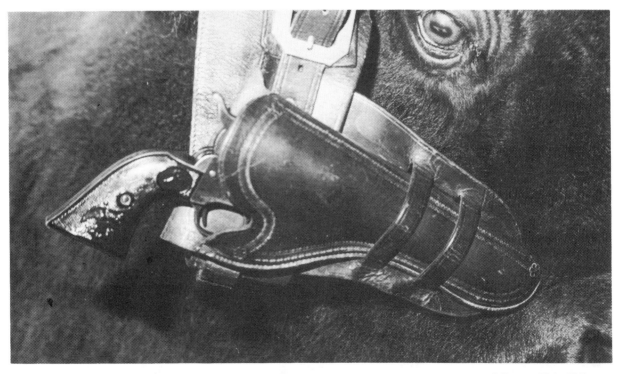

Collection of John W. Stewart

Colt, SN 95529, .44-40 cal., etch panel, 4 3/4 bbl., blue finish, shipped to Charles Hummel & Sons, San Antonio, Texas, March 19, 1885. Colt manufactured in 1883. Holster and money belt rig by Shelton Payne, El Paso, Texas. Rig hanging on horn of old buffalo.

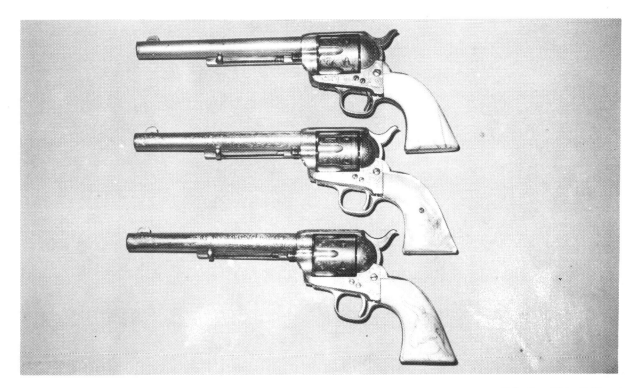

Collection of John W. Stewart

(A) (Top) SN 73294 .45 cal., shipped in the "soft" for engraving to Hartley & Graham, New York, N.Y., Oct. 12, 1881. (B) (Center) SN 159005, .44-40 cal., factory engraved nickel finish and shipped with eagle pearl stocks to Kitelsen & Degetem, El Paso, Texas, Nov. 16, 1894, in a shipment of one. (C) (Bottom) SN 75163, .44-40 cal., etched panel, shipped to Hartley & Graham, New York, N.Y., Dec. 31, 1881.

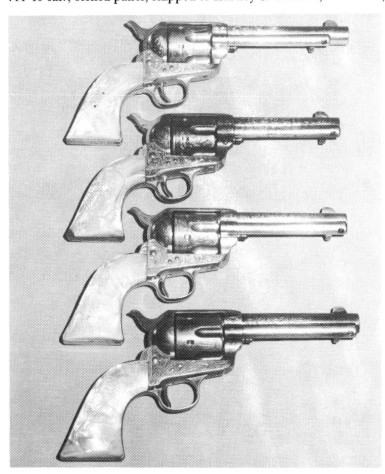

(A) (Top) SN 105747, .45 cal., factory engraved, nickel finish and shipped to Hartley & Graham, New York, N.Y., Aug. 21, 1884. (B) (Second from top) SN 185132, .38-40 cal., factory engraved nickel finish, and shipped with pearl ox head stocks to Louis Erhardt c/o J. A. Rose Atchison, Kansas, Jan. 2, 1900. Manufactured in 1899. (C) (Third from top) SN 92101, .44-40 cal., etched panel, shipped in the "soft" to Hartley & Graham, New York, N.Y., March 5, 1883. (D) (Bottom) SN 121226, .45 cal., factory engraved, blue finish, shipped to Hartley & Graham, New York, N.Y., April 14, 1887.

Collection of John W. Stewart

Colt, SN 95811 and 95927. Both Colts shipped in .45 cal., 4 3/4" barrel length with factory engraving and carved ivory bulls head stocks to A. J. Anderson, Fort Worth, Texas, July 30, 1885. Both in same shipment and manufactured in 1883. Holster rigs are marked F. A. Meanea, Cheyenne, Wyoming.

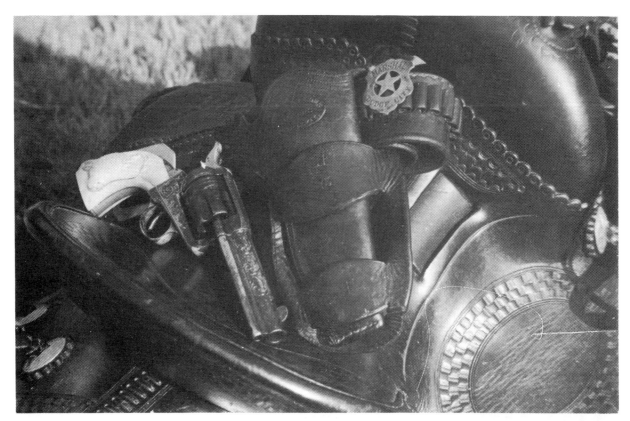

Colt, SN 185132, .38/40 cal., 4 3/4" bbl., factory engraved with nickel finish and factory pearl ox head stocks. Shipment of one to Louis Erhardt c/o J. S. Rose, Atchison, Kansas, Jan. 2, 1900. Colt manufactured in 1899. Holster rig marked L. Kiper & Sons, Atchison, Kansas.

Colt, SN 95211, .44-40 cal., etched panel, 4 3/4" bbl. Shipped with blue finish and wood one-piece grips to Newton & Andrews, El Paso, Texas, May 18, 1886. Shipped with shipment of one. Manufactured in 1883. Holster rig hallmarked Newton & Andrews, El Paso, Texas.

Collection of John W. Stewart

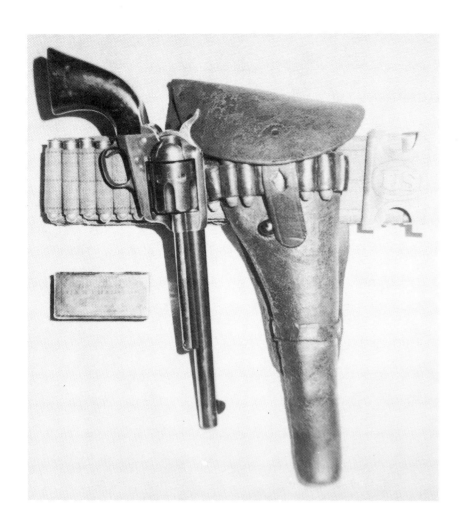

Collection of John W. Stewart
Colt Serial No. 116718, .45 cal., manufactured in 1885 U. S. Cavalry, David F. Clark inspected. Shown with the 1883 "Ropes Pattern" experimental holster and mills belt manufactured at the San Antonio Arsenal.

Collection of John W. Stewart
Colt Serial No. 124829 cal. .44/40 Etch Panel 4 3/4" barrel length, shipped with nickel finish and eagle rubber grips to R. J. Campbell October 11, 1888. Shown with holster rig marked S. C. Gallup, Pueblo, Colorado.

Colt, SN 159005, cal. .44/40, 7 1/2" bbl, factory engraved, nickel finish, shipped with factory pearl stocks to Kitelsen & Degetem, El Paso, Texas, Nov. 16, 1894. Holster money belt rig marked R. T. Frazier, Pueblo.

Collection of John W. Stewart

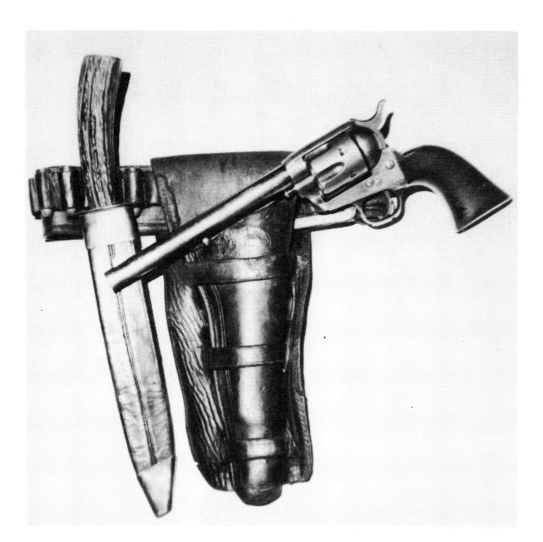

Collection of John W. Stewart
Colt Serial No. 40482. cal. .4[5]
7 1/2" barrel length. Shipp[ed]
with blue finish and wood gri[ps]
to J. P. Lower, Denver, Co[l.]
March 23, 1877. Shown wi[th]
holster rig marked Frazer [&]
Young, Durango, Col.

Collection of John W. Stewart
Colt Serial No. 121226. cal. .45 factory engraved with 4 3/4" barrel length and blue finish. Shipped to Hartley & Graham April 14, 1887. Shown with holster rig marked W. B. Ten Eyck, Billings, MT. (Montana Territory)

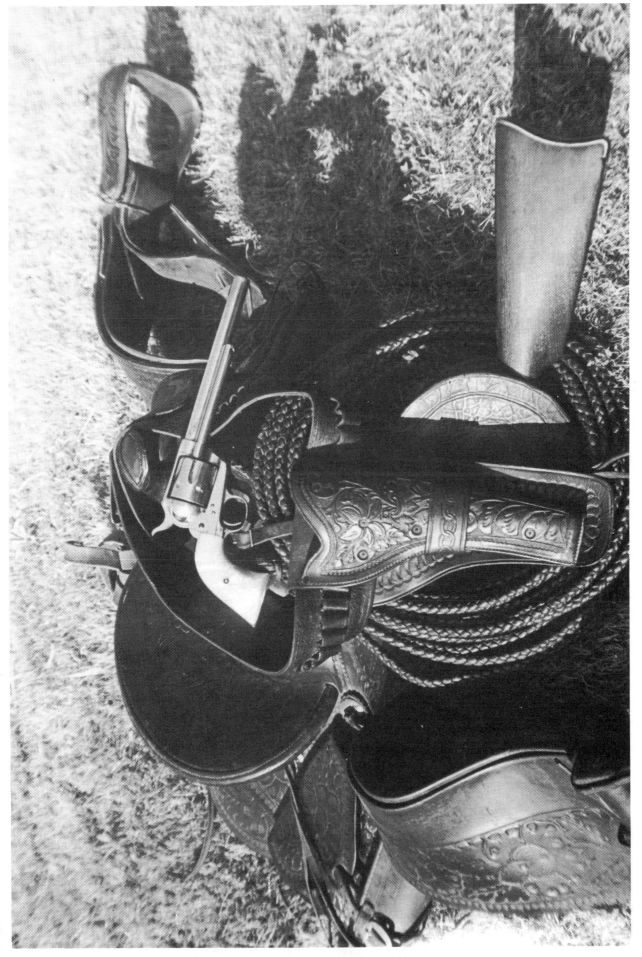

SN 143741, .45 cal., 7 1/2" bbl., nickel finish. Shipped to Colt Patent Firearms, San Francisco Agency, San Francisco, California, May 18, 1892. Holster and money belt rig hallmarked Visalia Stock Saddle Co., San Francisco, California.

Collection of John W. Stewart

Colt, SN 99106, cal. .44/40, etch panel, 4 3/4" bbl. Shipped with nickel finish and one piece wood grips to E. J. Post & Co., Albuquerque, New Mexico, in a shipment of one March 29, 1886. Colt manufactured in 1883. Holster rig marked El Paso Saddlery Co., El Paso, Texas.

Colt, SN 123295, .45 cal., 4" bbl., sheriff model. Shipped with nickel finish and eagle rubber stocks to Dunlay & Geisler, Houston, Texas, April 30, 1895. Colt manufactured in 1887. Holster marked A. H. Hess & Son, Houston, Texas.

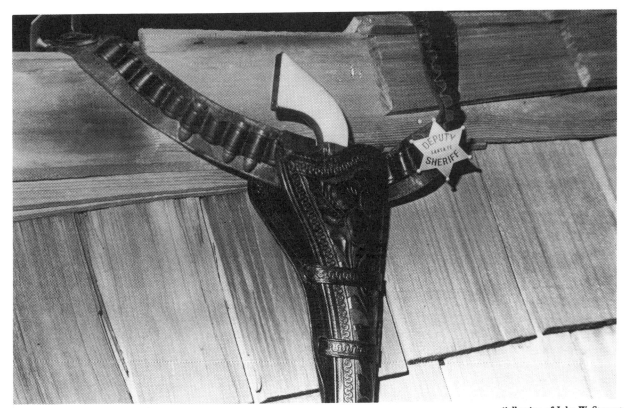

SN 52614. Colt cal. .44/40, etched panel, 7 1/2" bbl. Shipped with blue finish to Wexell & DeGress, Mexico City, Mexico, Sept. 1, 1879.

SN 67074. Colt .45 cal., 7 1/2" bbl. Shipped with nickel finish and wood grips. Grips stamped B. J. McCutcheon who was a rancher and worked with the Texas Rangers around the El Paso area. McCutcheon is mentioned in several old west books such as *Texas Guns & History* and *Border Boss*. Rig marked J. K. Polk, Sweetwater, Texas.

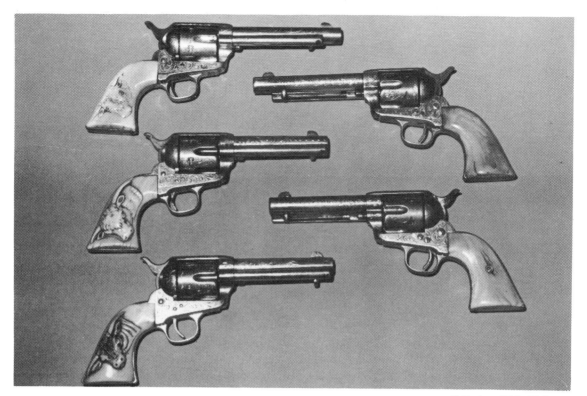

Collection of John W. Stewart

(A) (Top Left) - SN 73310, .45 cal., shipped in the "soft" for engraving to Hartley & Graham, New York, N.Y., Oct. 12, 1881. (B) (middlel left) SN 95927, .45 cal., factory engraved, nickel finish and shipped with carved ivory bulls head stocks to A. J. Anderson, Fort Worth, Texas, July 30, 1885. Manufactured in 1883. (C) (Bottom Left) SN 114194, .45 cal. factory engraved nickel finish and shipped with carved ox head ivory stocks to E. A. Worden, Dallas, Texas, Nov. 22, 1886. (D) (Top Right) SN 67028, .45 cal. shipped to Hartley & Graham, New York, N.Y., May 2, 1881. (E) (Bottom Right) SN 95811, .45 cal., factory engraved, nickel finish and shipped with carved ivory bulls head stocks to A. J. Anderson, Fort Worth, Texas, July 30, 1885. Manufactured in 1883. Note: B. and E. were shipped in same shipment.

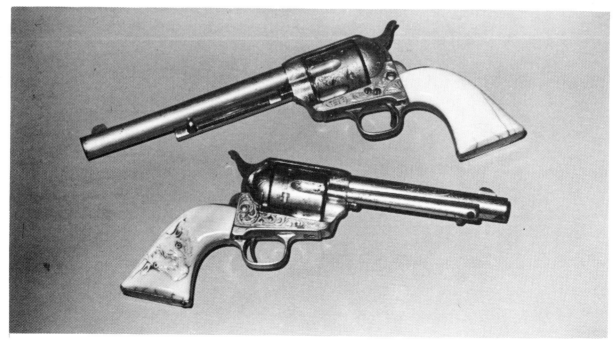

Collection of John W. Stewart

(A) (Top) SN 73294, .45 cal., shipped in the "soft" for engraving to Hartley & Graham, New York, N.Y., Oct. 12, 1881. (B) (Bottom) SN 73310, .45 cal., shipped in the "soft" for engraving to Hartley & Graham, New York, N.Y., Oct. 12, 1881. Note A & B shipped in same shipment.

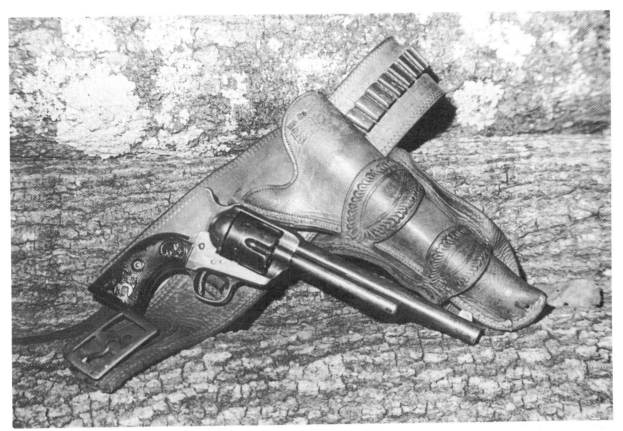

Collection of John W. Stewart

Colt SN 105957, .44-40 cal., etch panel, 7 1/2" bbl. Shipped to Manzanares & Co., Las Vegas, New Mexico, April 1, 1887. Colt manufactured in 1884. Holster and money belt rig hallmarked Denver Mfg. Co., Denver, Colorado.

Collection of John W. Stewart

Colt, SN 77612, .45 cal., 3 1/2" bbl, sheriff model, blue finish. Shipped to Hibbard, Spencer, Bartlett & Co., Chicago, Ill., Feb. 25, 1882, which was the first shipment of sheriff models. Colt pictured on page 68 in Kopecs book *A Study of the Colt Single Action*.

A few interesting items from the 101 Ranch Wild West Show and the 101 Ranch in Oklahoma.

The upper photo shows a top view of a typical performer's trunk used to carry costumes as the show toured the world.

The center photo is of a N.R. Davis 12 gauge double barreled shotgun serial #7841 marked as 101 ranch property. It may have been used in the show as well as on the ranch. It is sitting on a Millers Brothers 101 Ranch cowboy hat. These hats were distinctly marked inside with the 101 logo.

At left is a studio photo of a fully outfitted cowboy including a magnificent set of woolly chaps. This may be a real cowpuncher or it could as well be some dude in studio clothing having his photo taken at the Wild West show to impress the folks back home.

Photo by Rodney Yates

Collection of David Tate

SN 8630. Colt records show this .45 cal., 4 3/4" bbl. was shipped "in the soft" for engraving to Hartley & Graham, New York, NY, on Jan. 10, 1883. This was the personal sidearm of Texas Ranger and rancher Bill Curtis.

Bill Curtis & His Diamond Tails

Bill Curtis... Diamond Tails Ranch., both are synonymous with Texas.

Bill, or William Riley Curtis, had ancestors who fought in the American Revolution and one who signed the Declaration of Texas Independence. But Bill signed his brand on sixty thousand cattle.

As a boy he had learned to shoot with both hands with equal dexterity. That was all the deed to property he needed.

His childhood and young manhood were adventuresome. He was always amidst Indians, & freighters when barely in his teens, living through the War Between the States. Serving for a while as a Texas Ranger.

The Diamond Tails Ranch was located in several different areas of the Texas panhandle, including Jacksboro, Jack County, later in Clay County, Cache Creek.

Curtis died in 1901.

The present owner of Serial # 86930 bought the Colt Single Action directly from the family of Bill Curtis.

It is believed he bought the gun new.

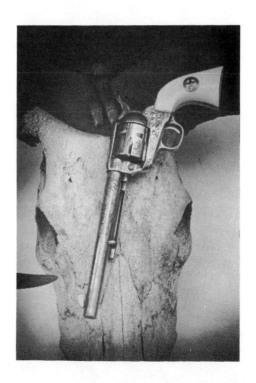

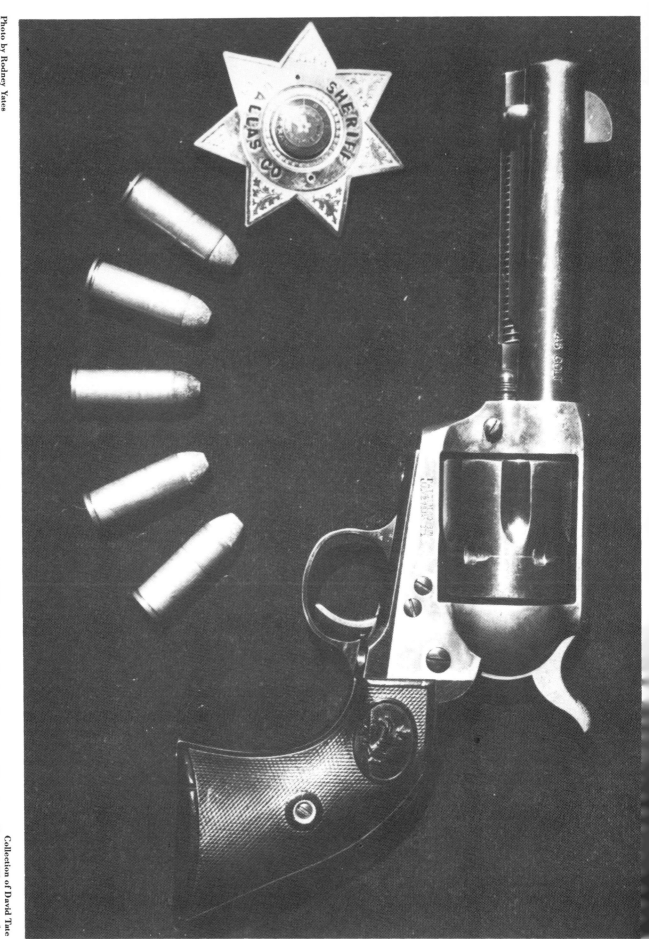

Photo by Rodney Yates
Collection of David Tate

Colt records indicate this .45 cal., 4 3/4" bbl. blue finish was shipped on August 30, 1922, to C. L. Bering Company, Houston, Texas. This was the personal revolver of Bill Decker, Sheriff of Dallas County, Texas from 1949 till his death on August 29, 1970. The five cartridges were in the gun at the time of his death. SN 343474.

Bill Decker
Sheriff, Dallas County
Dallas, Texas

Bill Decker began his lawman career in 1923 as a deputy constable. He later served 14 years as chief deputy of Dallas County, Texas. In 1948 Decker was elected sheriff and was never challenged again at the polls. He died in office at the age of 71.

Some of the things Decker is best known for...
- The role he played in the capture of the
  notorious bank robbers Bonnie & Clyde
- His capture of Raymond Hamilton, a Texas badman
- The role he played after the Kennedy assassination...
  and later testified before the Warren Commission during their investigation

Long before the Kennedy assassination Decker had amassed numerous honors and was considered the outstanding sheriff in the Southwest. Sheriff Decker is considered by many to be the last of the old frontier-type lawmen.

According to Deputy Sheriff Vester Lee (Butch) West, the Colt .45 Single Action, Serial #343474 was one of Decker's favorite guns.

Photo by Rodney Yates — Collection of David Tate
SN 351138. This .45 cal., 4 3/4" bbl. blue finish was shipped on Oct. 18, 1927, to San Antonio Police Dept., San Antonio, Texas. Note factory markings on butt S.A.P.D. No. 35. Shown with contemporary San Antonio #35 badge.

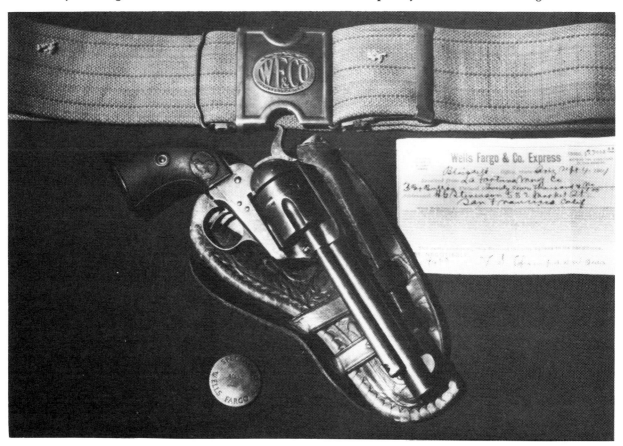

Photo by Rodney Yates — Collection of David Tate
SN 285678. This .45 cal., 5 1/2" bbl. blue finish revolver was shipped on Nov. 12, 1906, to Wells Fargo Co., New York, N.Y. Factory markings on butt W. F. & Co. Pictured with the gun is a Mills Mfg. Wells Fargo belt & buckle.

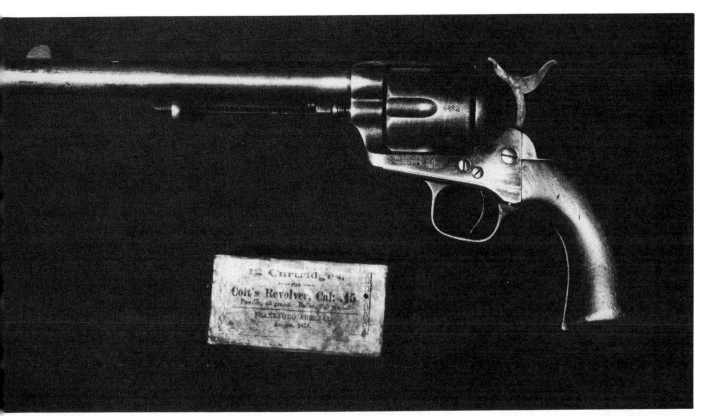

N 6682. Although there is no factory record on this U.S. revolver, it came from a collection in Montana. The U.S. Calvary was the ultimate law and order in the early west. Shown with the .45 cal., 7 1/2" bbl. U. S. is a box of .45 ammo mfg. August, 1874.

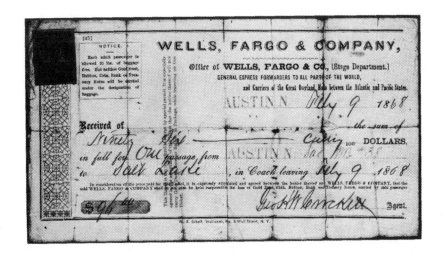

Shown here and on the cover is a magnificent 101 Ranch show saddle and bridal. It is beautifully tooled and features both nickel and silver decorations. The Saddle horn is marked "101 RANCH". This type of rig would be used by the Miller brothers in the parade when the show came to town and in the actual show.

SN 224478, .45 cal., 4 3/4" bbl., Ivory Grips. Shipped to Krakauer, Zork & Moye, El Paso, Texas, on April 4, 1902.

Collection of G. R. Taylor

SN 230851, .38-40 cal, Shipped to Bering Cortes Hardware, Houston, Texas on August 15, 1902.

Collection of G. R. Taylor

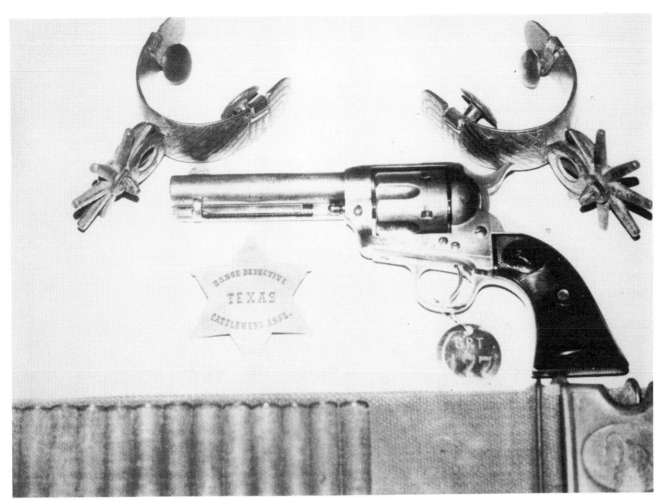

Photo by G. R. Taylor
Collection of G. R. Taylor

SN 258080, cal. .38-40, 4 3/4 inch barrel, rubber grips. Shipped to Ed. S. Hughes & Co. Abilene, Texas on Sept. 6, 1904. Shown with contemporary Texas Cattlemens Assn., Range Detective badge and Anson Mills rifle cartridge belt/buckle and hammered silver inlayed spurs. circa 1885.

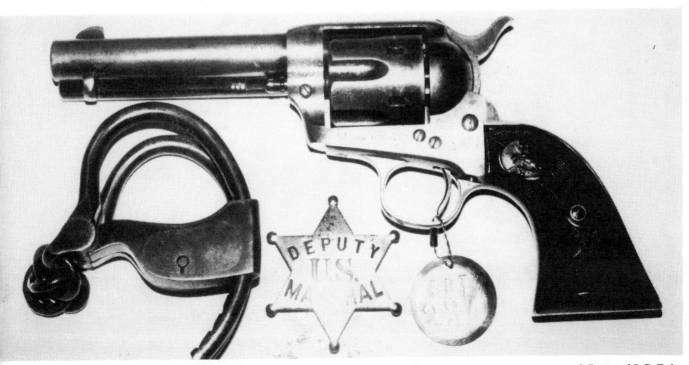

Photo by G. R. Taylor
Collection of G. R. Taylor

SN 260330, cal. .32-20, 4 3/4 inch barrel, rubber grips. Shipped to Walter Tips, c/o W. B. Fox, Austin, Texas on November 4, 1904. Shown with contemporary deputy U.S. Marshal badge and Tower handcuffs, circa 1890.

SN 283506, cal. .45 LC., 4 3/4 inch barrel, rubber grips, Shipped to Bering Cortes Hardware Co. Houston, Texas on Oct. 10, 1906. Shown with C. M. Russel Bronze of Will Rogers, circa 1923.

SN 195608. This .44-40 cal. 7 1/2" bbl., left the Colt factory on April 20, 1900 bound for Lee, Glass, Anderson Hardware, Co., Omaha, Nebraska. Shipment of one. The rubber grips are original but are not listed on the factory letter. Shown with contemporary holster & belt marked George Tritch Hdwe. Denver, Colorado.

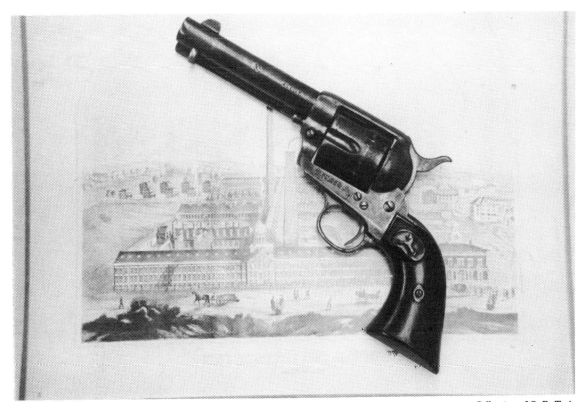

Collection of G. R. Taylor

SN 243846, .45 cal., 4 3/4" bbl., Colt factory in background. Shipped to Jackson & Hughes, El Paso, Texas, on August 17, 1903.

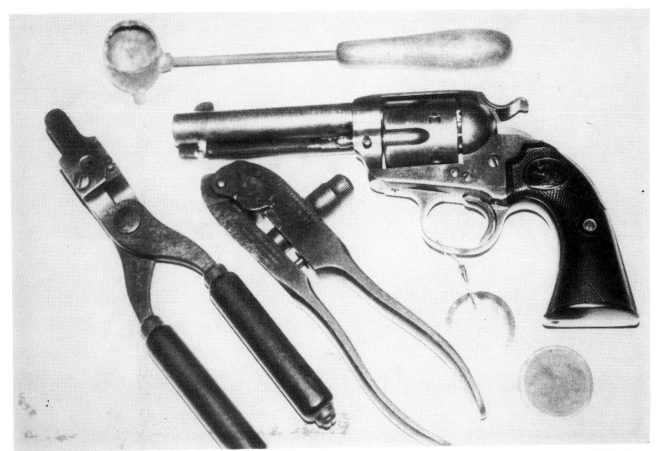

Photo by G. R. Taylor Collection of G. R. Taylor

SN 256376, cal. .44-40 Frontier Six Shooter, 4 3/4 inch barrel, rubber grips. Colt Bisley model revolver. Shipped to Dunham, Carrigan & Hayden Co., San Francisco, California on July 29, 1904. Shown with contemporary .44-40 loading tools, circa 1885.

Photo by G. R. Taylor
Collection of G. R. Taylor
SN 175137, cal. .44-40, Frontier Six Shooter, 5 1/2 inch barrel, Ivory Grips, Shipped to Colt's Patent Firearms Co. San Francisco Agency, on February 5, 1898. Shown with playing cards, poker chips, and dice. Circa 1898.

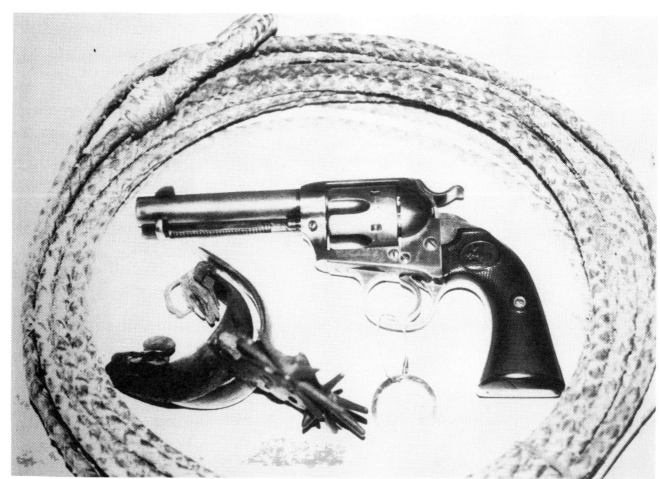

Photo by G. R. Taylor
Collection of G. R. Taylor
SN 213394, cal. .45 LC., 4 3/4 inch barrel, rubber grips, Bisley model. Shipped to Charles Hummel Fire Arms Commerce Street, San Antonio, Texas, on August 14, 1901. Shown with contemporary rawhide lariot and spurs, from Texas, circa 1880. Ranch Brand AP carved in left grip, registered to Alfred Pfullmann, for Cattle, on May 13, 1908, in Wilson County Texas.

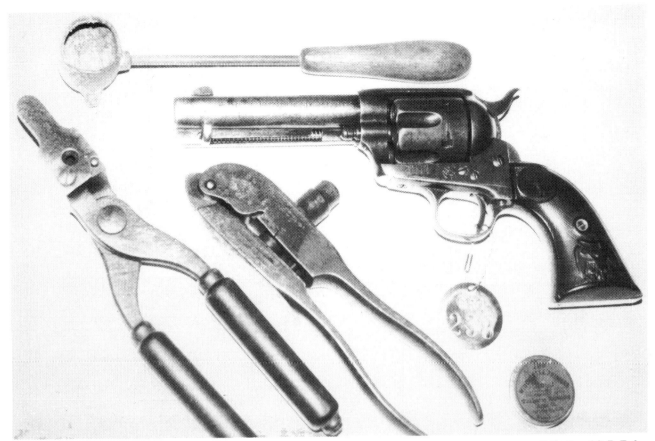

Photo by G. R. Taylor
Collection of G. R. Taylor
SN 135156, cal. .44-40 Frontier Six Shooter, 4 3/4 inch barrel, eagle rubber grips, shipped on Aug. 30, 1890, to Hibbard, Spencer, Bartlett & Co., Chicago, Illinois. Shown with contemporary .44-40 loading tools, circa 1885.

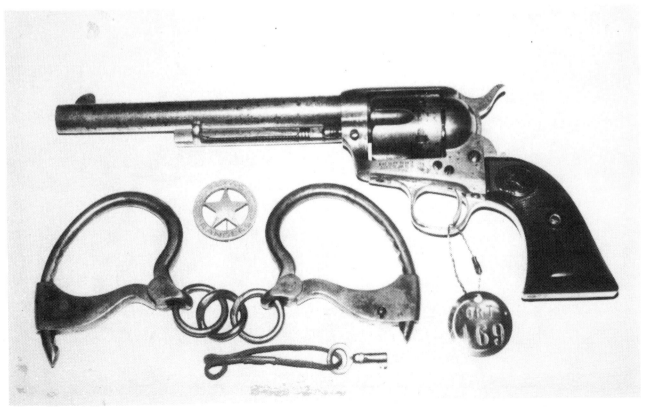

Photo by G. R. Taylor
Collection of G. R. Taylor
SN 174130, cal. .45 LC. Nickel Finish, 7 1/2 inch barrel, rubber grips. Shipped to Walter Tips, Austin, Texas on May 13, 1898. Shown with contemporary Texas Ranger Badge and Tower Handcuffs circa 1880.

Indian Wars weapons presented to members of the 7th cavalry. At the top is a converted military trade breechloader serial #710. This smoothbore carries a silver presentation plaque reading "Taken from White Lance at The Battle of Wounded Knee December 29th, 1890 - Presented to Major Samuel Whitside 7th U..S. Cav." The lower is a Colt 1883 10 gauge double bbl. shotgun, serial #2571. The receiver is engraved "Presented by the Officers and Men of the 7th U.S. Calvary" on the left side and "Capt. Winfield S. Edgerly April 26, 1889" on the right. The trigger guard is engraved with crossed sabers and the number 7. Edgerly was present at both the Little Big Horn and Wounded Knee battles.

Whitside and Edgerly appear in the Wounded Knee group photo shown below.

Officers of Seventh Cavalry who participated in the battle of Wounded Knee, S.D., 1891

Civil War Military Issue Sharps Rifles and Carbines. From the top; New Model 1859 Percussion Carbine serial #64168, New Model 1863 Percussion Carbine serial #20621, New Model 1863 Percussion Carbine conversion to metallic cartridge, serial #27876 and New Model 1859 Percussion Rifle serial #55948. This rifle was issued in the summer of 1862 to the famed 1st Regiment U.S.. Sharpshooters commanded by Col. Hiram Berdan.

A Civil War Confederate 12 ga. double bbl.. shotgun used as a guard weapon to protect a bridge from Yankee marauders. Shotgun is marked " C.S." on the right side of the stock. Shown with it is a document relating to guarding the bridge and a tintype of the intrepid Confederate guards with their shotgun. It was not unusual for the South to press any type of weapon into service as it had little production capacity and was forced to depend on imported and captured weapons.

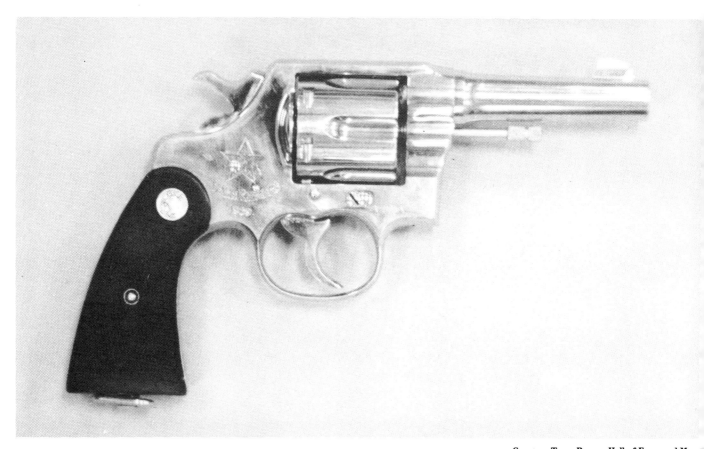

Courtesy Texas Ranger Hall of Fame and Muse

FRANK HAMER'S COLT .38. This Colt .38 Special Serial # 346706 was presented to Captain Frank Hamer by the State Texas in 1939.

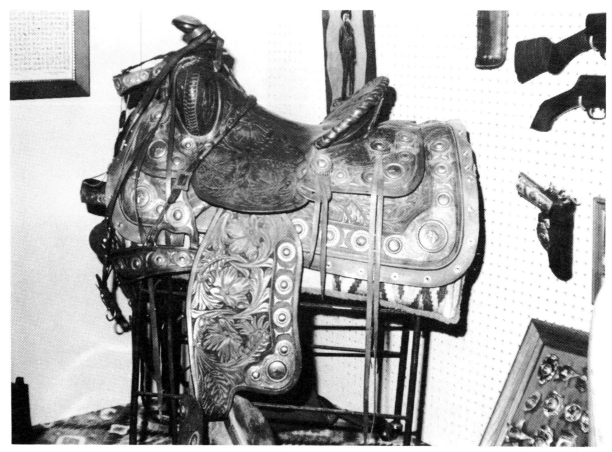

Courtesy Texas Ranger Hall of Fame and Museum

PARADE SADDLE. This is one-of-a-kind manufactured by Keyston Bros. of San Francisco, California.

CAPTAIN BILL McDONALD'S ENGRAVED COLT SINGLE ACTION. This Colt .45 was owned by Ranger McDonald and later by Captain Clint Peoples. McDonald died January 15, 1918.

Close-up view of McDonald's Colt.

TEXAS RANGER TOM HICKMAN'S ENGRAVED COLT SINGLE ACTIONS. Hickman served as Captain of Co. B during the 1920-1930s. He became a captain in 1921 and was chairman of the Public Safety Commission when he died in 1962.

TEXAS RANGER HARRISON HAMER'S COLT SINGLE ACTION. This pearl-handled Colt .45 and single loop holster w[as] used by Ranger Hamer during the 1930s.

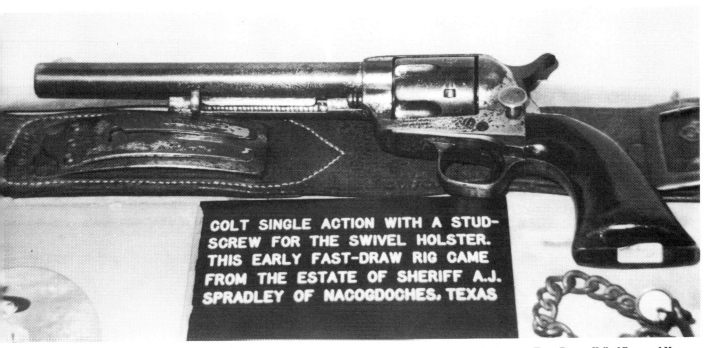

SHERIFF A. J. SPRADLEY'S COLT SINGLE-ACTION with stud screw for swivel holster. This early outfit was used for fast draw. Spradley was sheriff at Nacagdoches, Texas.

TEXAS RANGER DAN WESTBROOK'S RIFLE AND SIDEARMS.

Courtesy Texas Ranger Hall of Fame and Museum

CAPTAIN JOHN R. HUGHES" ENGRAVED COLT SINGLE ACTION. Hughes served as Captain of Company D from 1893 until his retirement in 1915. He was stationed in El Paso for several years.

Courtesy Texas Ranger Hall of Fame and Museum

SPECIAL RANGER L. J. CANAFAX'S COLT BISLEY .45. This Bisley was carried by Canafax during his tenure as Special Ranger and U. S. Revenue Officer.

Shown on the trunk are Zack Miller's 101 Ranch Wild West Show cowboy hat and a Worthington Arms Co. 12 gauge double bbl. hammer shotgun with 30" fluid steel bbls., serial #188576. It is marked 101 Ranch on the receiver and buttstock. It was used on the ranch or in the Wild West show.

Two unusual souvenir items from the 101 Ranch Wild West Show. The sombrero is coin or sterling silver and is marked "101 Ranch" on the front of the crown. (see inset at left).The scarf which is very colorful, features four Indian Chiefs and is embroidered with the show's name.

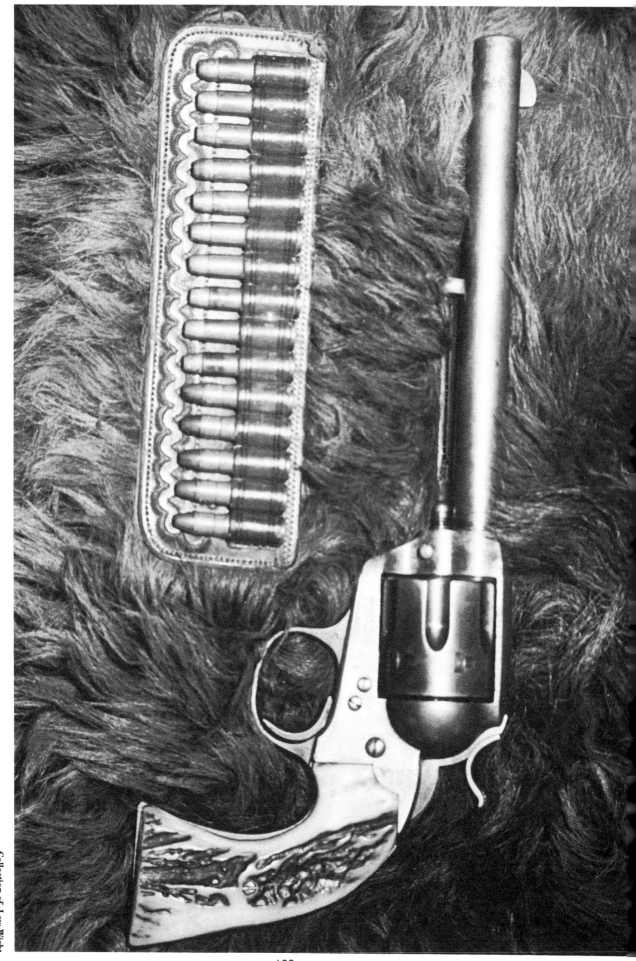

SN 302272. This .32-20 cal., 7 1/2" bbl, Bisley Model, blue finish, firearm was shipped December 23, 1907, to Blish, Mize & Silliman Hardware Co., Atchison, Kansas. Shipment of one. A notarized statement from a New Mexico State Police Supervisor states this revolver was shot by Mexican Bandit Pancho Villa and the last six hollow point cartridges shown in the leather cartridge clip were replaced by Villa himself. NOTE: Most guns in this collection were photographed on a buffalo hide.

Collection of Lew Wight

N 171352 (top) and 186043 (bottom) The Special Target Model .45 cal. was shipped March 2, 1898, to Hibbard, Spencer, Bartlett & Co., Chicago, IL. This Bisley was carried by U. S. Marshal Ben Collins who was killed in the line of duty in 1906. The .38-40 cal. nickel finish was factory engraved and shipped July 6, 1899, to Roberts, Sanford, & Taylor Co., Sherman, Texas, with carved steerhead pearl grips. This Bisley was used by three generations of U.S. Marshals in Oklahoma. Dan Collins, brother to Ben, (1837-1921) Charlie Collins (1885-1969) and George Collins (1909-1982). They are shown with the leather they were carried in during their use in Indian Territory.

N 160045. This .45 cal. 4 3/4" bbl. was inscribed at the factory, L. S. HOPE in German script and shipped to him in 1895. The holster shown is a fine single loop, narrow skirted, wrap-around loop, unmarked, but possibly of Texas origin.

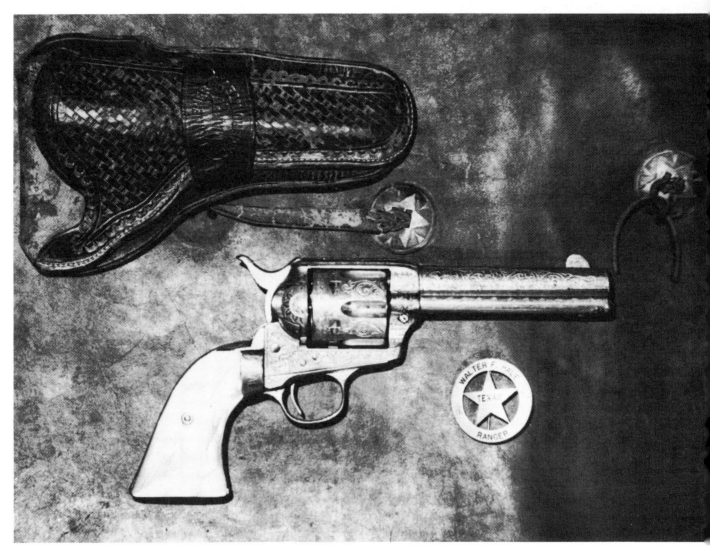

Collection of Lew Wi[g]

Walter F. Hale's Colt 45 SAA

SN 221374. This .45 cal., 4 3/4" bbl., engraved with carved pearl American Eagle grips was the personal sidearm of Tex[as] Ranger, Walter F. Hale, Sr. Before becoming a Ranger in 1918, Hale was City marshal in Belton, Texas. The pistol was given him in 1912 by the citizens of Belton. He carried the pistol while city marshal of Belton, and also when he was a road mast[er] working for the railroad. He was a Texas Ranger and joined the Rangers in 1918. He later passed the Colt pistol down to h[is] son, Walter Fleetwood Hale Jr. Walter Jr. was a city policeman in Waco, Texas in the late 1920's and in the early 1930's [he] became the city marshal of Calvert, Texas. While he was the city marshal of Calvert, he shot and killed a man by the name [of] Cantrell, who had robbed the Bank of Calvert. He also shot and seriously wounded a man by the name of Emmons who w[as] Cantrell's partner in the bank robbery. Both men were shot with the Colt pistol. Walter Jr. collected a five thousand doll[ar] reward for killing the bank robber. Mr. Hale then joined the Texas Rangers and was stationed in Marfa, Texas. While he was [a] ranger, he and two other rangers were indicted for killing a man by the name of Prieto. The trial was moved to another coun[ty] on a change of venue and Walter Jr. and the other two rangers were acquitted of this charge. Hale served in World War II a[nd] after the war he joined the Border Patrol and was stationed in San Benito. At the time of Hale's death, he was a speci[al] investigator for the State Insurance Company. He carried the Colt pistol with him constantly from the time it was given to hi[m] in the late 1920's until the early 1950's, when it was finally retired. No factory record is available.

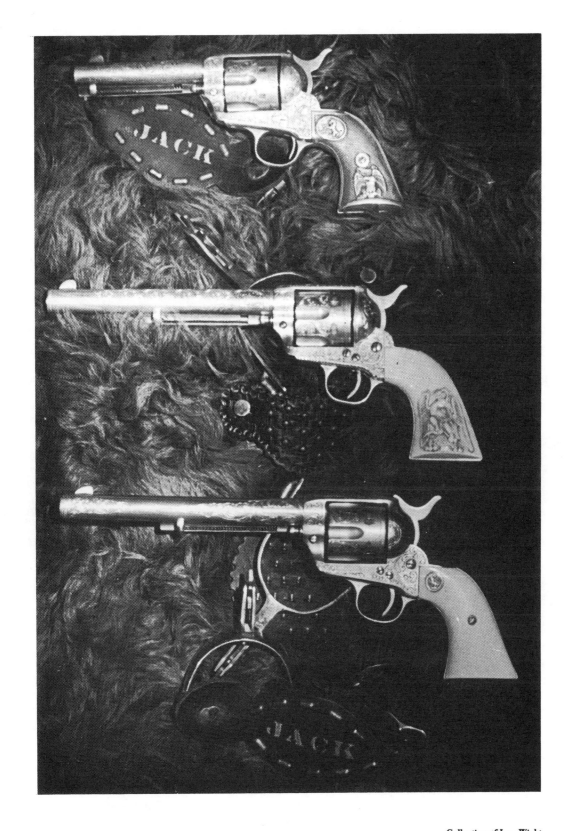

Collection of Lew Wight

SN 323566 (top) SN 304972 (middle) SN 305035 (bottom). These Colts were used by rodeo performer Jack Case. The top gun is a .32-20 cal., 4 3/4" bbl., manufactured in 1912. Stamped under the solid silver grips are the words The 101 W.W.S. The middle gun is a .45 cal., 7 1/2" bbl., Factory engraved with carved ivory grips given to Case by Buck Taylor, also a rodeo performer. This, according to his wife, was one of his favorite guns. The bottom gun in photo is also a .45 cal., 7 1/2" bbl., Factory engraved with ivory medallion grips, manufactured in 1908. Also shown in photo are chaps & spurs from the Jack Case Wild West Show. Case was also with The 101 Ranch Wild West Show.

Collection of Lew Wi[...]

F. H. Lancaster's Colt SAA 45

SN 155296. This .45 cal., 5 1/2" bbl, factory engraved, revolver with Mexican Eagle carved pearl grips was shipped to S[an] Antonio, Texas in 1894. At that time, it was engraved on the backstrap "F. H. Lancaster" and was silver plated. It is al[so] possible that the Mexican Eagle carved pearl grips were also added at this time. Mr. Lancaster's career as a "lawman" is a ve[ry] lengthy one. He was born in 1862 in Mountain View, Arkansas, and left home at the age of 18, in 1881 to locate in Colora[do] City, Texas. He worked there as a Cowboy for the Champion Cattle Co. for some time. He then was appointed Deputy Sher[iff] under Dick Ware, a famous Texas lawman since he killed outlaw Sam Bass at Round Rock, Texas. While working with War[e,] Lancaster became a friend as well as a knowledgeable lawman. When Ware was appointed U. S. Marshal of the Weste[rn] District of Texas, headquarters near San Antonio, in 1893, Lancaster went with him to serve as Deputy U. S. Marshal. F. [H.] Lancaster held this position for Ware, and his successors George Seibricht and Marshal Nolte. In the 1890's, Lancaster s[aw] much action in the Garza Revolution; an incident which involved violation of neutrality laws because Garza organized alo[ng] the Rio Grande near Brownsville to attack on the Mexican side. Lancaster was credited with the plan that captured the lead[er] of this group. In 1910, Fred left the U. S. Bureau of Investigation. He served as Chief of Police of San Antonio from 1913-192[0.] From 1920-1934 Lancaster served as a Special Investigator for the city of San Antonio. In 1934, he was given a spec[ial] commission and was involved in The Texas Rangers, at the age of 72.

Collection of Lew Wight

Tex Perry's Cattle Brand Colt SAA

SN 7988. This .45 cal. began its history as a 7 1/2" bbl., U. S. Calvary and was manufactured in 1874, the second year of production. It was undoubtedly used in the Western Indian Wars. After the transition from a Calvary Colt to the shortened 5 1/1" bbl., Artillery, the old Colt became a cowboy's sidearm. Some of the ranch markings on #7988 are: "IXL" (Texas), "101" (Oklahoma), "E" (T.E. Ranch), "d" (Rocking D Ranch), "–20" (Bar 20 Ranch), "◇E" (Diamond E), "Ọ" (Running O Ranch), and "5" (Lazy 5 Ranch). It was then engraved with the owner's name on the backstrap "Tex Perry", and silverplated and fitted with 1911 Double Die Rampant Colt Medallion Ivory grips. The holster and cartridge belt is unmarked and are of the type made up at the local saddle shops and sold by mail order through Sears and Montgomery Ward.

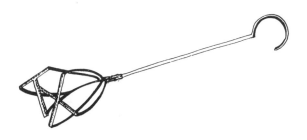

Collection of Lew Wight

William J. McDonald

William Jesse McDonald was born in Mississippi in 1852 and came to Texas with his family in 1866.

His career as a lawman included serving as sheriff of Wood County, deputy sheriff, Special Ranger and U. S. Deputy Marshal for the Northern District of Texas, and the Southern District of Kansas. He became Captain of Company B, Frontier Battalion, in 1891. He and his company worked such cases as the Wichita Bank Robbers, the Wichita train strike, the Murder Society of San Saba and the Humphreys murder mystery. In 1905 he was appointed bodyguard to President Theodore Roosevelt while Roosevelt was in Texas. He investigated U. S. Troops after the Brownsville Riot, and later served as a state revenue agent. In 1912 he was bodyguard for Woodrow Wilson, who later appointed him U. S. Marshal for the Northern District of Texas.

McDonald died in Wichita Falls, Texas on January 15, 1918.

Legendary for his audacious courage, it was said that "Bill McDonald would have charged Hell with a bucket of cold water."

Remington SA #297. This beautifully engraved Remington Single Action was the personal sidearm of Bill McDonald, Captain, Texas Rangers. Shown here with the Remington are the original holster and a book written about the many exploits of Ranger McDonald. Engraved on the top side of the barrel is W. J. "Bill McDonald" Texas Ranger Captain.

Collection of Lew Wight

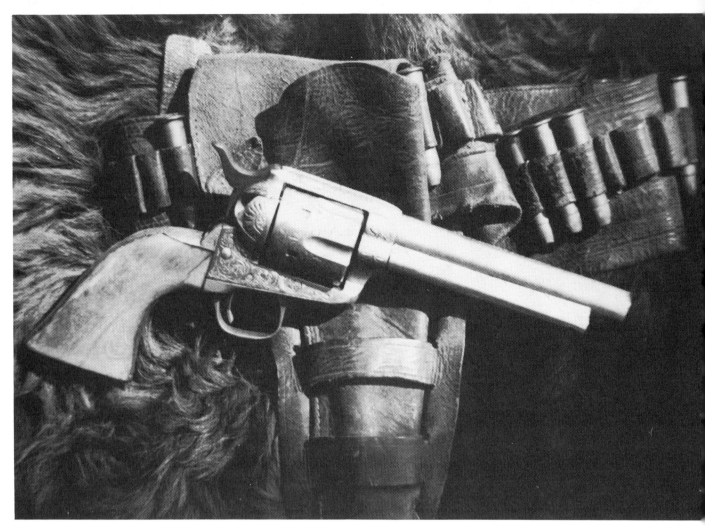

Collection of Lew Wig[...]

Frank Mills "Texas Ranger" Colt SAA

SN 27794. This .45 cal. was manufactured in 1876, the 3rd year of production. This firearm was a 5 1/2" bbl. has one-pie[ce] ivory grips, and was shipped to H. D. Folsom Arms Co., a New York dealer. The history for the next 47 years is unknown. [In] 1923 Texas Ranger Frank Mills picked up 27794 from the ground near Del Rio, Texas, after a gun battle with some Mexica[n] cattle rustlers.

This firearm was carried by Frank Mills through a long career of law enforcement: Del Rio, Texas, Co. A. Rang[er] Force, 1923-1925; Sheriff, Coleman County, Texas; and again Ranger Co. Headquarters, Coleman, Texas, 1937-1939. Mil[ls] then gave the old Colt to his son, Billy Mills, sheriff of Crockett County, Texas. Billy then gave the gun to Bob Caldwell, deputy sheriff of Crockett County. The holster is a Mexican double-loop, and the belt is looped for .40-60 cal. ammo. This is [a] typical Ranger outfit of that era.

Collection of Lew Wight

N 348480. This .45 cal., 5 1/2" bbl., blue finish revolver left the Colt Factory December 7, 1925. According to the Factory ter, R. J. Brady, was the person receiving the shipment of one. Documents accompany the firearm which suggest it was a gift Tom Brady, Texas Ranger, Company D. Brady served with Captain William L. Wright (1868-1942).

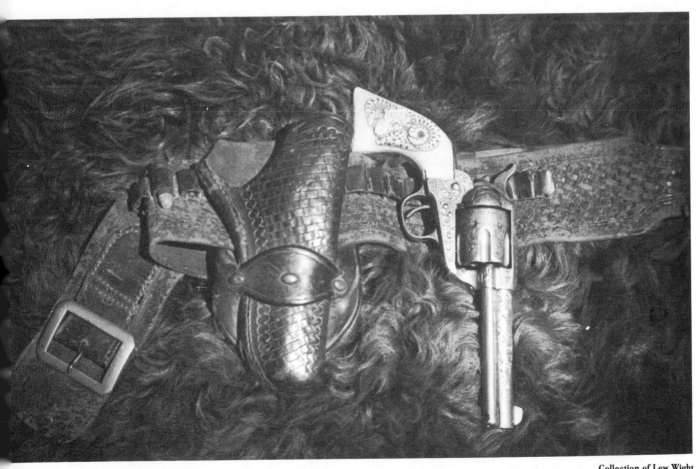

Collection of Lew Wight

N 87903. This .44-40 cal., 4 3/4" bbl., was shipped "in the soft" for outside engraving to Hartley & Graham, New York, New rk on February 17, 1883. The carved Rams Head pearl grips were probably fitted by the New York dealer.

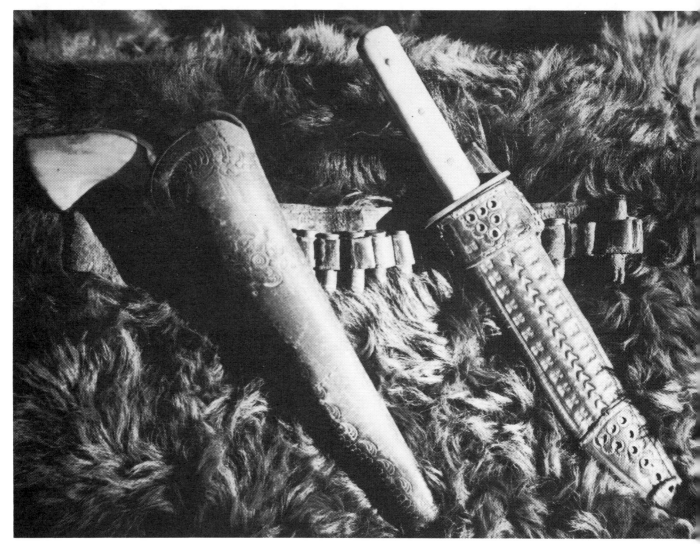

Collection of Lew W

Colt SAA & Bowie Knife Rig

SN 77573 and Bowie Knife Rig. This revolver, .44-40 cal., etched panel, 7 1/2" bbl., nickel plated with one-piece ivory gr was manufactured in 1882. The rig has the Early Missouri Line Holster, the second variation of the 1860 Army Flap Hols This was the most commonly used holster during the late 1860s and 1870s. The Bowie Knife is ivory handled and the scabb is marked on the back, "From old Mexico on Feb. 1879" and a name which is now illegible. The belt has many old a corroded .44-40 cartridges.

Collection of Lew Wight

N 136748. This .44-40 cal. 7 1/2" bbl., nickel finish with pearl grips (all confirmed in letter from Colt Factory) was shipped on January 10, 1891, to J. Bielenberg, Brownsville, Texas. This Colt Frontier Six Shooter is in superb condition.

Collection of Lew Wight

350675. This .45 cal. 4 3/4 bbl., blue finish revolver was shipped November 17, 1927, to City of San Antonio, Texas, Police Dept. Fifty in shipment. Factory engraved on the backstrap is S.A.P.D., #90 on butt. The holster is a Furnstnow's "Sheriff's Lightning Spring Shoulder Holster."

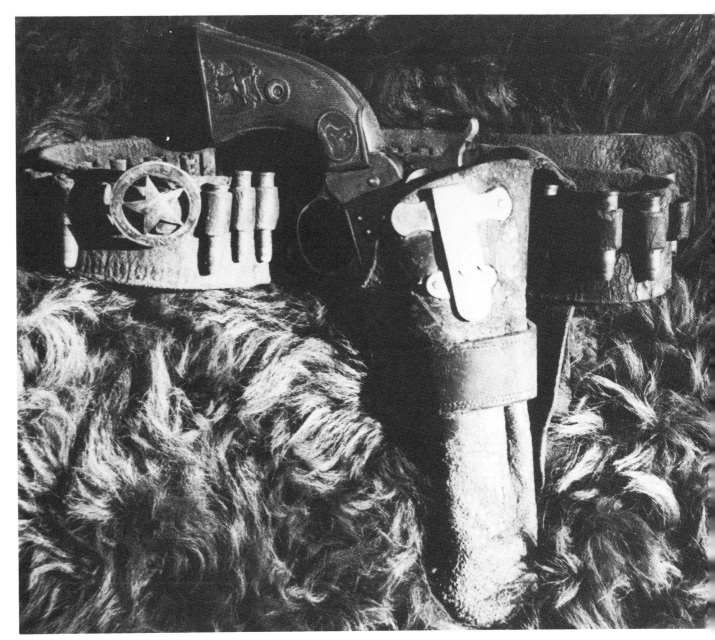

Collection of Lew Wi[?]

Jules Baker "Texas Ranger" Colt S.A.A.

SN 332544. This .32-20 cal., 4 3/4" bbl., was made in 1916 and has hard rubber "Eagle Grips". It was owned by "Tex[as] Ranger" Jules Baker. The various law enforcement jobs he held were: Deputy Sheriff, Mitchelle County, Colorado City, Tex[as]; Texas Ranger, 1907, Co. A Ranger Force, Colorado City, Texas; Brand Inspector, 1920; Texas Ranger, Co. A. Ranger Forc[e] Presidio County, Station, Texas, 1922-1924. The rig he wore in 1916 as a Ranger and Brand Inspector is a "Bringham Paten[t] Holster and cartridge belt. The holster has the "waist band clip" that allows the holster to be worn off the belt, inside t[he] pants, and under neath the shirt for concealment purposes. The .32-20 and .25-20 cal. ammo in the cartridge belt is typical [of] the Texas Rangers.

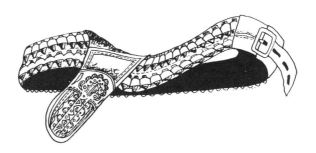

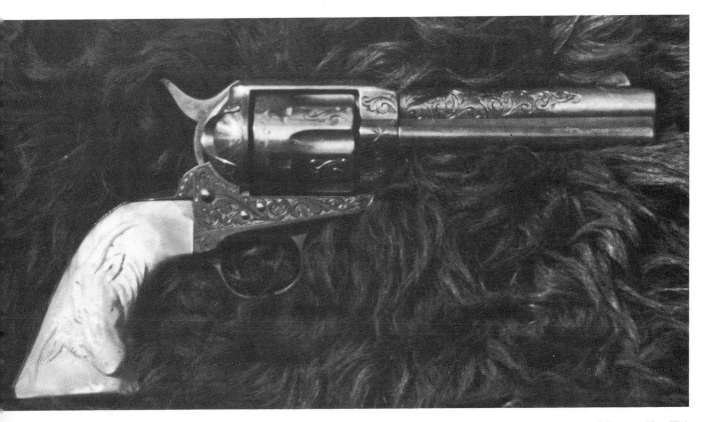

275496. This .45 cal., 4 3/4" bbl. Silver finish, pearl carved steerhead left the factory bound for W. S. Cox, no address. The letter states that C. A. Farnsworth, Sheriff, Grant County 1905-06 is engraved on the backstrap. Later research shows that this was Silver City, New Mexico.

275496. Left side view showing the beautiful pattern of Colt engraving during this period. This firearm was shipped in 1906.

Collection of Lew Wight

SN 324629. This .45 cal. 4 3/4" bbl. factory engraved (B style) fitted with pearl grips was shipped in 1912 to Praeger Hardware, San Antonio, Texas. Special order shipment of one. This was the personal sidearm of Dick Hickman (1917-1951), Chief of Police, Colorado City, Texas. The fine hand tooled Mexican double-loop holster is marked "HYB VERHELLE, BROWNSVILLE, TEXAS.

Collection of Lew Wight

SN 121135. This U.S. Artillery was shipped from the factory to the U.S. Government in 1887. Later it was used by Reeder Webb, Sheriff, Ector County, Odessa, Texas, for 18 years (1923-1941). The tooled holster is marked S.D. MYERS, EL PASO, TEXAS. Other items of Sheriff Webb are his jail keys, leather lead-shot filled hand club and aluminum knuckles.

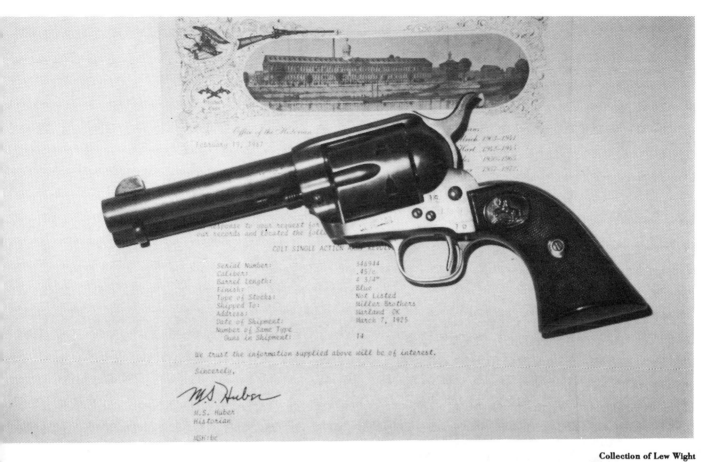

SN 346944. This .45 cal., 4 3/4" bbl., blue finish firearm was shipped directly to the 101 Ranch (Miller Bros.) in Marland, Oklahoma, March 7, 1925.

Photo of the Miller Brothers of 101 Ranch fame. L-R: Zach, J.C., and George L. Made in Marland, Oklahoma during the mid-twenties.

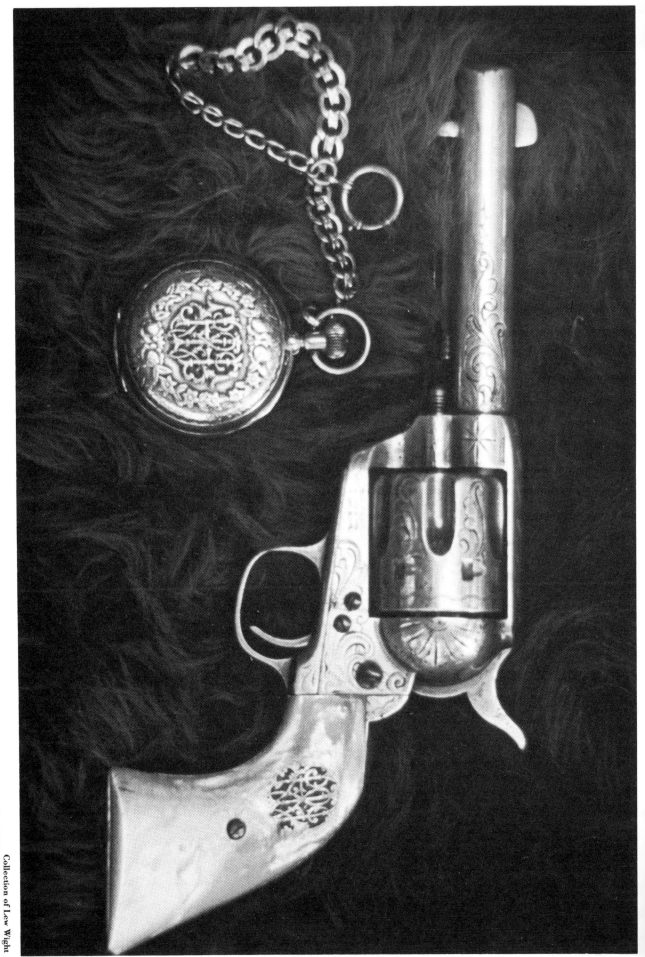

SN 110874. This .45 cal., 4 3/4" bbl., Factory engraved, silver finish revolver was shipped August 9, 1884, to Hartley & Graham, New York, N.Y. Shipment of six. According to the factory records no stocks were on the Colt when it was shipped. Note the monogram HJW on the pearl grip and matching HJW on watch. Inside the watch is the inscription, H.J. Ware, Del Rio, Texas. The history of this beautiful Colt is now being researched.

Collection of Lew Wight

SN 62751 (left) Colt Cobra .38 Special Light Weight and SN 23887 (right) Colt Cobra .38 Special Light Weight.

Clint Peoples, U. S. Marshal
Northern District of Texas

These service revolvers were issued to Texas Ranger Clint Peoples in 1940, by The Texas Department of Public Safety, and has DPS markings. They were used by Peoples during his illustrious law enforcement career in Texas. He served as Deputy Sheriff, Special Texas Ranger, Chief Deputy Constable, Chief Deputy Sheriff, Texas Highway Patrolman, Texas Ranger Private, Captain, Texas Rangers, and finally U. S. Marshal. The revolvers are pictured with his I.D. Cards and a portrait of Peoples which hangs on a wall at The Texas Ranger Hall of Fame and Museum in Waco, Texas. Peoples retired in 1986.

Rusty relics have a character all their own. This .45 cal., Black Powder relic was found fully loaded in 1901 by a hunting party including President Taft in Sturgis, South Dakota. Note the Eagle grips.

This relic is a .32-20 Black Powder in the 160,000 range was found on a Houston, Texas street by a road construction crew. The hammer is down on empty while the remainder of chambers are loaded.

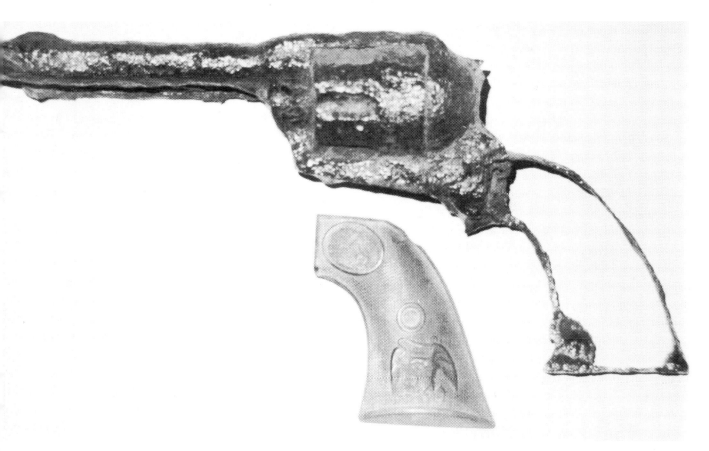

Collection of Lew Wight

This .38-40 cal. relic was found fully loaded in the desert sixteen miles east of Bisbee, Arizona at Double-A-Dobe. Note the condition of the eagle grip.

Collection of Lew Wight

This .45 cal., 4 3/4" bbl., Serial # 155343 relic was found in Texas near the Rio Grande. It has what appears to be the original one-piece walnut grips. The diamond-shaped inlay is ivory.

Collection of Lew Wight

SN 36978. This .45 cal., 7 1/2" bbl. was manufactured in 1877. According to documents on July 20, 1878, Texas Sheriff Moore shot and wounded Texas outlaw Sam Bass with this weapon at Round Rock, Texas.

Shown on this page are three 101 Ranch Cowboy hats, a horse bit found in the 101 trunk featured on the cover and a Rickard 12 gauge double barrel hammer shotgun.
The shotgun having 22" barrels and serial #51374 is marked "101 Ranch" and was used a working gun on the ranch in Oklahoma or in the 101 Ranch Wild West Show.

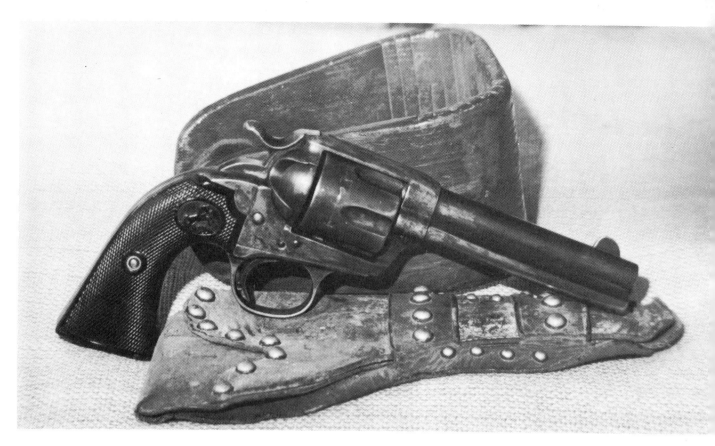

SN 211205. This .41 cal., 4 3/4" bbl., blue finish Bisley model was shipped June 29, 1901, to Krakauer, Zork & Moye Co., El Paso, Texas. Shipment of five. Pictured with old wooden stirrup and double-loop studded holster.

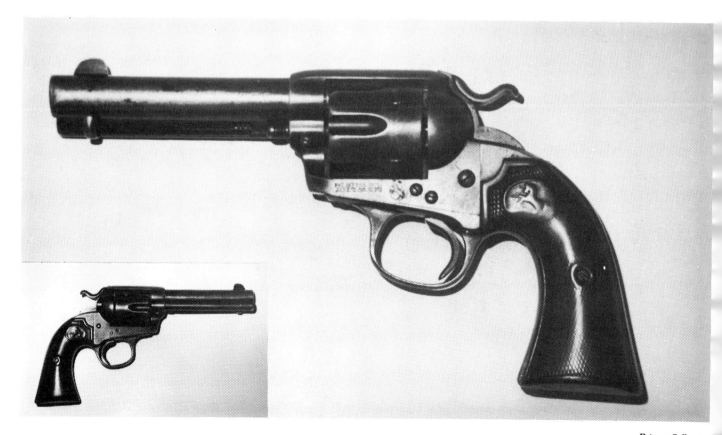

SN 263803. This .41 cal., 4 3/4" bbl., blue finish Bisley model was shipped May 1, 1905, to Krakauer, Zork & Moye Co., El Paso, Texas. Shipment of four.

Private Collection

N 344877. This .45 cal., 4 3/4" bbl., nickel finish revolver was shipped Feb. 3, 1923, to Wolf & Klar, Fort Worth, Texas. Shipment of one. The engraving was done by Wolf & Klar before leaving there and the pearl grips were probably added much later.

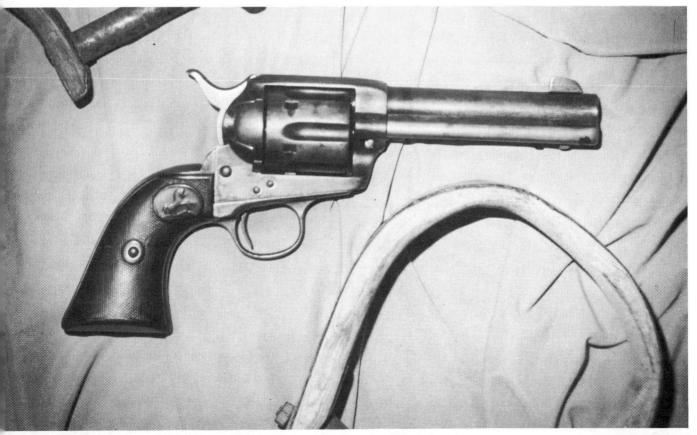

Private Collection

N 330888. This .45 cal., 4 3/4" bbl., blue finish, Long Flute Model was shipped August 11, 1915, to Bering Hardware Co., Houston, Texas. Shipment of three.

SN 114692. This Texas Colt letters "all the way." The .45 cal., 4 3/4" bbl., nickel finish was factory engraved and shipped June 30, 1885 to A. J. Anderson, Fort Worth, Texas. Shipment of one. The letter also states the grips were carved Bull Head Ivory.

SN 114692. Left side view showing grade B engraving.

Private Collection

N 255955. This .38-40 cal., 5 1/2" bbl., blue finish revolver was shipped June 29, 1904, to Bering-Cortes Hardware Co., Houston, Texas. Shipment of three. The nice pearl grips are replacements. Shown with some Texas badges.

Private Collection

N 289676. Colt factory records indicate this .44-40 cal., Colt Frontier Six-Shooter, 5 1/2" bbl., Bisley Model, blue finish was shipped February 22, 1907, to Krakauer, Zork & Moye, El Paso, Texas. Shipment of twelve.

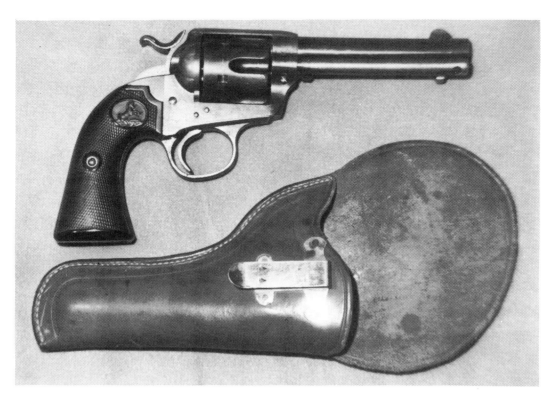

Private Collection

SN 177995. This .45 cal., 4 3/4" bbl., blue finish Bisley model left the Colt factory May 17, 1898, (Antique) bound for Charles Hummel & Son, San Antonio, Texas. Shipment of one. Shown with Waist-Clip holster marked "S. D. MYRES, SWEETWATER, TEXAS."

Private Collection

SN 271271. This .41 cal., 4 3/4" bbl. revolver was mfg. in 1905. No factory information is available. Shown here with old doubleloop holster marked "J. K. POLK, SWEETWATER, TEXAS" on back.

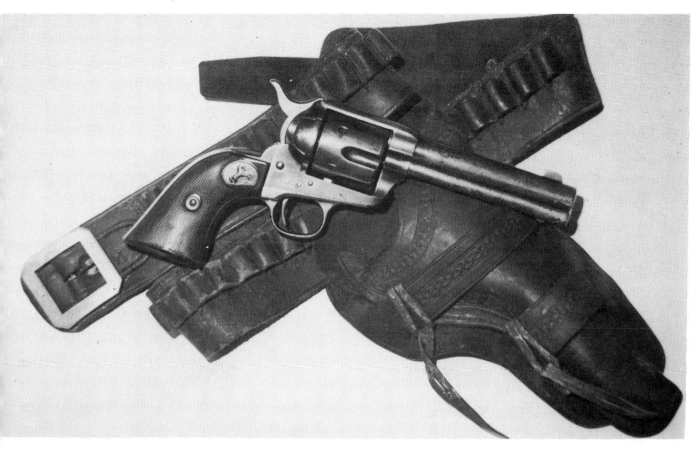

N 143876. This .41 cal., 4 3/4" bbl., blue finish revolver left the factory Nov. 24, 1891, bound for Charles Hummel & Son, San Antonio, Texas. Shipment of five. Shown with old double-loop holster & belt.

N 136888. This .45 cal., 4 3/4" bbl., blue finish revolver was shipped January 7, 1891, to E. A. Worden & Co., Dallas, Texas. Shipment of four.

Private Collection

SN 270723. This .45 cal., 4 3/4" bbl., blue finish Colt was shipped October 2, 1905, to Walter Tips Co., Austin, Texas. Shown with old basket weave holster marked "J. C. Madeley, Jr., Maker, Conroe, Texas," and old Colt 1878 double-barrel shotgun.

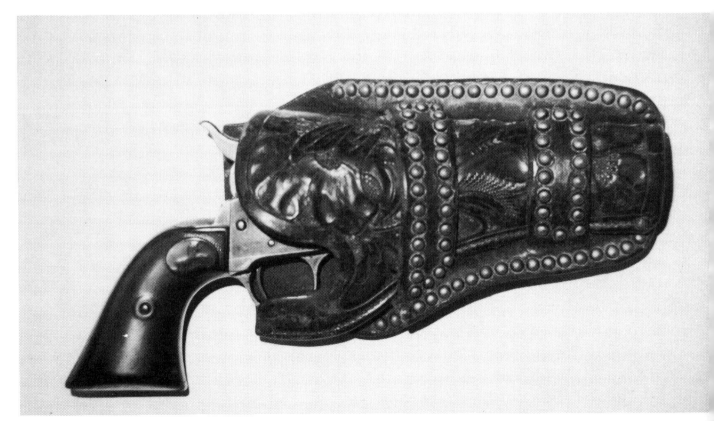

Private Collection

SN 187064. This .45 cal., 4 3/4" bbl., blue finish revolver left the Factory June 27, 1899, destined for Walter Tips Co., Austin, Texas. Shown in hand-tooled studded double loop holster marked "H. H. HEISER, Denver, Colorado."

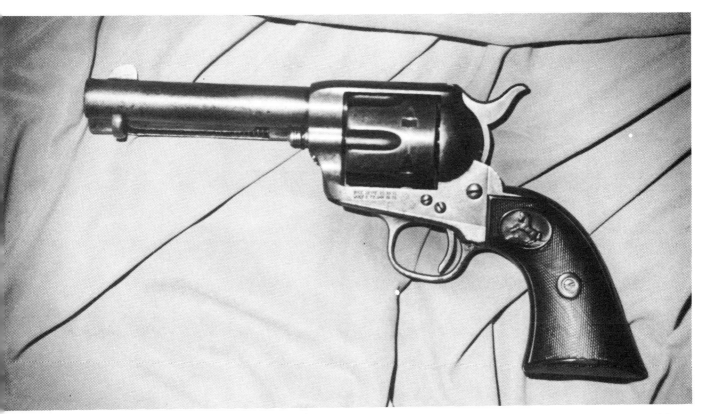

Private Collection

N 157657. Although this .44-40 cal., 4 3/4" bbl., blue finish six-shooter was shipped August 6, 1894, to Hibbards, Spencer, Bartlett & Co., Chicago, Illinois, it still has Texas history. It was owned many years by Gaines deGraffenried, Curator at The Texas Ranger Hall of Fame and Museum in Waco, Texas.

Private Collection

N 139040. Colt records show this .41 cal., 4 3/4" bbl., nickel finish revolver was shipped August 1, 1891, to Walter Tips, Austin, Texas. Shipment of four. The pearl grips are not original to the gun.

Private Collection

SN 101473. This .45 cal., 4 3/4" bbl., blue finish revolver was shipped June 18, 1887, to Manzanares & Co., Las Vegas Territory of New Mexico. One hundred in shipment. This Colt left the factory with one-piece walnut grips, but now has ivory.

Private Collection

SN 293787. This .45 cal., 4 3/4" bbl., blue finish revolver was shipped May 4, 1907, to Copper Queen Consolidated Mining Co., Bisbee, Arizona. Five in shipment. Two chunks of Copper are behind the old leather belt and holster.

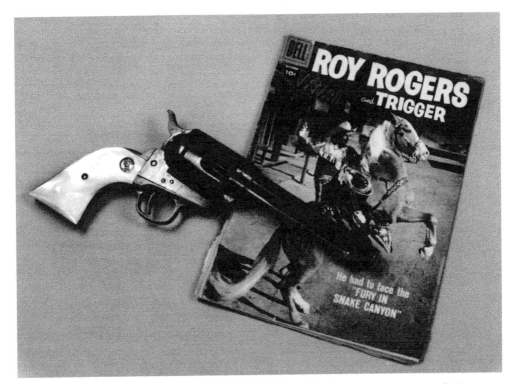

Colt Single Action, 41 caliber, 5&1/2" bbl. Serial #199869. This old Colt was a favorite of Roy Rogers, "The King of the Cowboys" and was used by him for many years.

Colt Single Action, 4&3/4" bbl. Serial #129194. This factory engraved revolver was owned and used by Texas Ranger Hugh Miller. His name is engraved on the backstrap. The badges were also his as documented by his family.

Colt Single Action, 45 caliber, 4&3/4" bbl. Serial #308018. The factory letter states that this nickel plated, factory engraved revolver was equipped with the unusual carved eagle pearl grips with ruby eyes. It was shipped on December 12, 1908 to Gonzales & Schafer in Laredo, Texas.

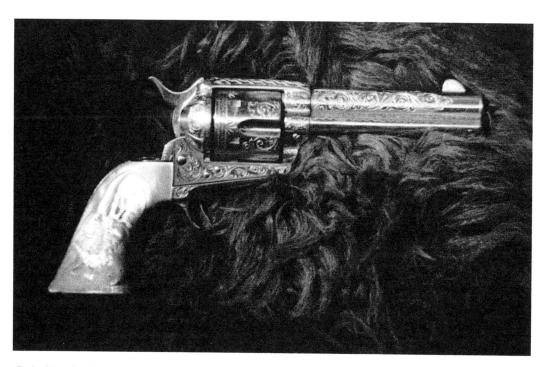

Colt Single Action, 45 caliber, 4&3/4" bbl. Serial #229902. This factory engraved nickel plated revolver with carved steerhead pearl grips was shipped on July 22, 1902 to Walter Tips Company in Austin Texas. Note the unusual partial trigger guard.

N 238587. This .38-40 cal., 5 1/2" bbl., nickel finish, Bisley Model was shipped Jan. 28, 1903, to Bering-Cortes Hardware ., Houston, Texas. Shipment of six. The pearl grips are not original to this Colt.

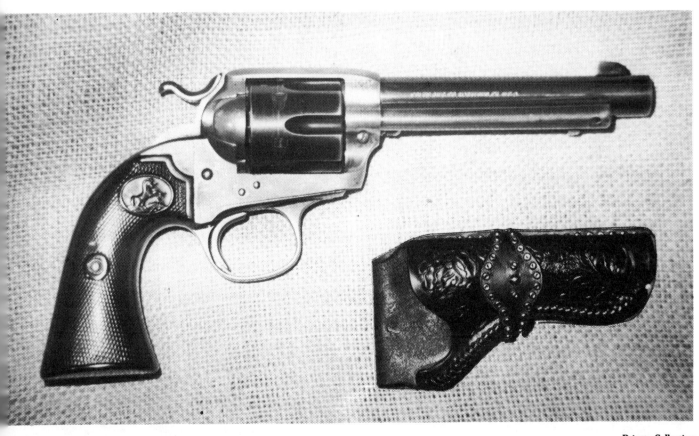

N 279242. This .38-40 cal., 5 1/2" bbl., blue finish, Bisley Model was manufactured in 1906. No factory record is available, t documents accompanying this revolver show that it was owned and used by a Jackson Hole, Wyoming Deputy Sheriff.

SN 214430. This .41 cal., 4 3/4" bbl., blue finish, left the Colt Factory September 6, 1901, bound for Walter Tips, Austi Texas. Shipment of two.

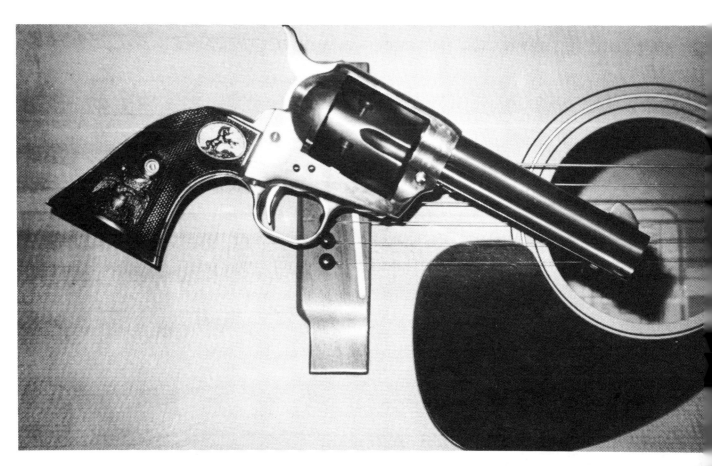
SN SA53627. This .44-40 cal., mfg. in 1981 was once a part of the Country & Western singer Hank Williams, Jr. collection.

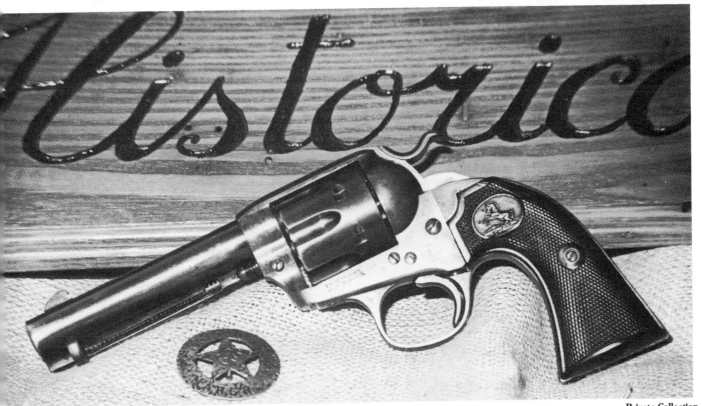

Private Collection

N 315570. This .32-30 cal., 4 3/4" bbl., blue finished revolver was manufactured in 1915 and was used by H. L. Sanderson, Norman, Oklahoma. It is inscribed "H. L. Sanderson, Norman, Okla." on butt. Sanderson was City Marshal there from 1913 until 1919.

Private Collection

N 213041. This .44-40 cal., 4 3/4" bbl., blue finish Colt Frontier Six-Shooter was shipped August 20, 1901, to Ed S. Hughes, Abilene, Texas. Shipment of seven.

Photo of El Paso Saddlery taken in 1899. This company was started in 1889 and remains in business today. Photo courtesy El Paso Saddlery.

Private Collection

Private Collection

SN 231372. Colt ledgers show this .44-40 cal., 4 3/4" bbl., blue finish Frontier Six-Shooter was shipped August 26, 1902, to El Paso Saddlery, El Paso, Texas.

SN 231372. Shown in early El Paso Saddlery marked holster. Note Indian-head nickel.

Private Collec[tion]

SN 139790. This .44-40 cal., Colt Frontier six-shooter, 4 3/4" bbl., nickel finish left the Colt factory April 10, 1891, for Char[les] Hummel & Son, San Antonio, Texas. Shipment of ten.

Private Collec[tion]

SN 330124. This .45 cal., 4 3/4" bbl., blue finish, long flute revolver was shipped August 25, 1913, to Shelton-Pay[ne] Hardware Co., El Paso, Texas. Shipment of six. The factory letter states this firearm was shipped with a double-acti[on] cylinder (long flute).

SN 248005. This .38-40 cal., 4 3/4" bbl., blue finish Colt left the Factory September 26, 1903, bound for Walter Tips Co., Austin, Texas. Shipment of five. Shown with old leather belt and holster. Although the holster is unmarked it is probably an A. W. Brill, Austin, Texas.

N 251255. This .44-40 cal., 4 3/4" bbl., Colt Frontier Six-Shooter was shipped February 18, 1904, to Kraukauer, Zork and Ioye Company, El Paso, Texas. Shipment of 10.

SN 250080. This .45 cal., 4 3/4" bbl., blue finish Bisley model revolver was shipped Dec. 11, 1903, to Bering-Cortes Hardware Co., Houston, Texas.

SN 150195. This .45 cal., 4 3/4" bbl., blue finish revolver left the Colt factory February 16, 1893, bound for Roberts, Willis Taylor & Co., Sherman, Texas. Three in shipment.

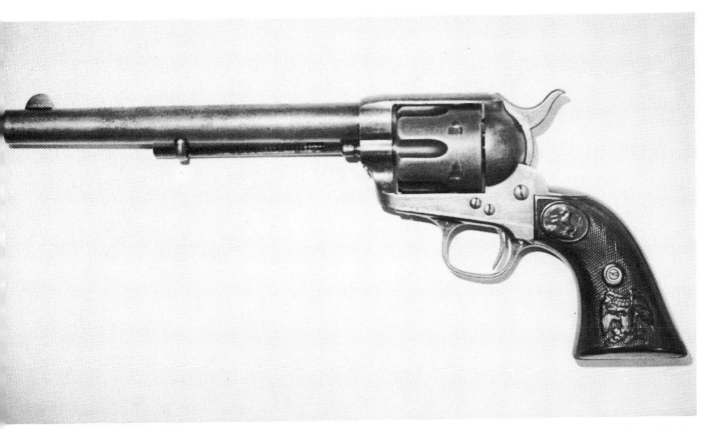

N 132401. This .45 cal., 7 1/2" bbl. with eagle grips was owned and used by S. J. Ivy, U.S. Deputy Marshal in the Kansas-Oklahoma Territories from 1890 until the early 1900s. According to family history S. J. Ivy was also a Confederate Soldier.

N 147062. This .45 cal., 4 3/4" bbl., blue finish revolver was shipped July 21, 1892, to Walter Tips, Austin, Texas. Shipment of three. This Colt has much of the original finish remaining.

Private Collection

SN 319706. This .45 cal., 5 1/2" bbl., blue finish revolver was manufactured in 1911. It was used by Texas Ranger Chell M. Baker during the early 1920s with Captain Will Wright, Co. D, in Laredo, Texas. The badge shown was also used later when he served as Special Ranger with the Santa Fe Railroad.

Colt and Winchester Texas Ranger Set. This .45 cal., 5 1/2", Serial # 319706, and Winchester Model 95 SRC, Serial #401812, .30-06 cal. were used by Texas Ranger Chell M. Baker. Baker served with Company D under Captain W. L. Wright in the early 1920's. Both the Winchester and Colt were modified for Ranger service by J. F. "Buster" Kreuz, a well-known gunsmith. Both weapons are marked "J. F. Kreuz, Austin, Texas." Baker was a peace officer spanning a fifty year period including service with the Santa Fe Railroad, the Brown County sheriff's office, and as a Special Texas Ranger. Also pictured is the holster and an old railroad badge (center of wagon wheel) used by Ranger Baker.

SN 319706. Top of barrel showing "J.F. Kreuz, Austin Texas" marking.

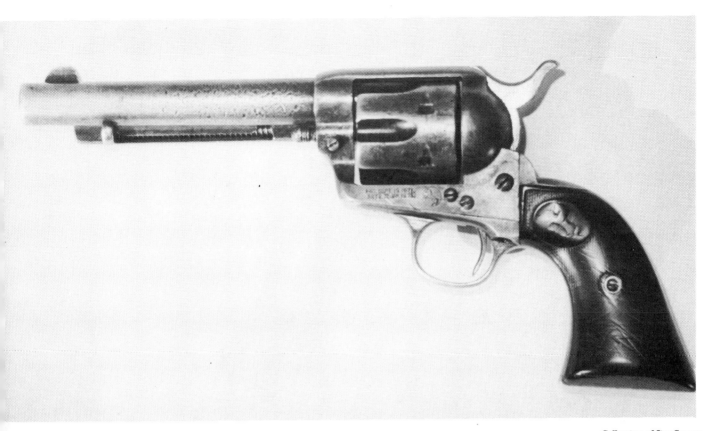

SN 214816. This .45 Colt, 5 1/2" bbl., blue finish revolver was shipped September 18, 1901, to Walter Tips, Austin, Texas. An affidavit with this Colt states it belonged to western movie actor Rod Cameron.

Collection of Jim Gossett

Rod Cameron, right, in scene from 1944 movie, "The Old Texas Trail."

Private Collection

SN 246739. Only a few Single-Actions were shipped to Abilene, Texas. This .41 cal., 4 3/4" bbl., blue finish revolver was shipped August 10, 1903, to Edward S. Hughes, Abilene, Texas. Shipment of ten. According to Colt records Mr. Hughes received a total of thirty weapons. Ten .38-40, ten .41, and ten .45 calibers. All were 4 3/4" barrel length. Much of the original finish remains on this revolver.

SN 220890. This .45 cal., 4 3/4" bbl., blue finish revolver was shipped January 24, 1902, to Krahauer, Zork, & Moye, El Paso, Texas. Old liquor bottle was dug in 1950 from Cripple Creek, Colorado dumping ground. Gambling chips, glasses, and dice also came from there. Shown with 41 Cal. Colt Derringer.

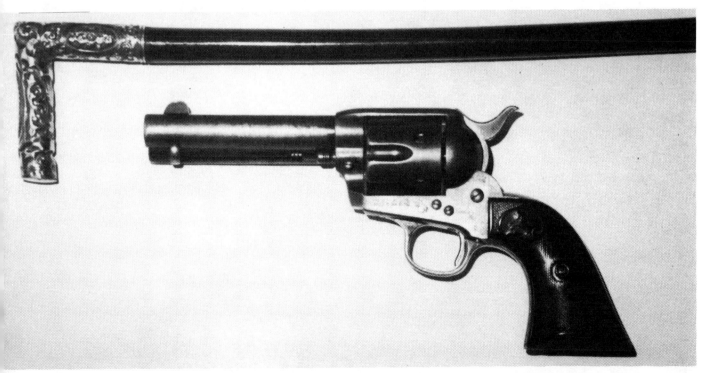

SN 261502. This .38-40 cal., 4 3/4" bbl., blue finish Colt was shipped December 5, 1904, to Roberts, Sanford, & Taylor Co., Sherman, Texas. Shipment of ten. Shown with contemporary walking cane with gold-plated handle marked "R. Barr, M.D., From Julia." on top.

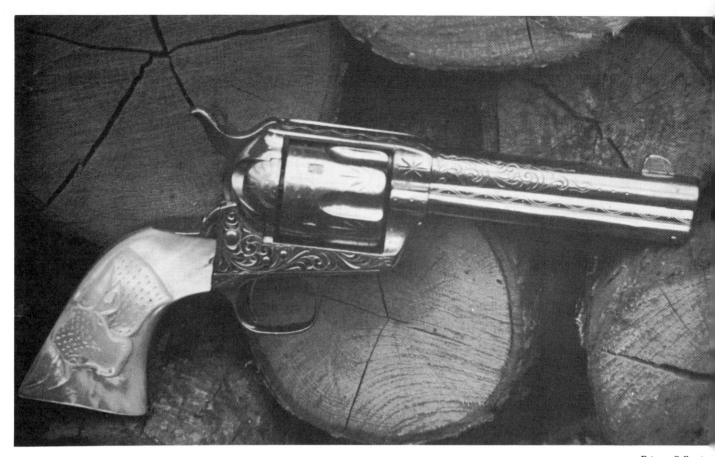

SN 117097. This .45 cal., 4 3/4" bbl., nickel finish revolver was factory engraved and shipped to J. C. Petmecky, Austin Texas, on March 4, 1886. Shipment of six. The carved steerhead pearl grips are later replacements.

SN 117097. Left side view showing the grade B engraving.

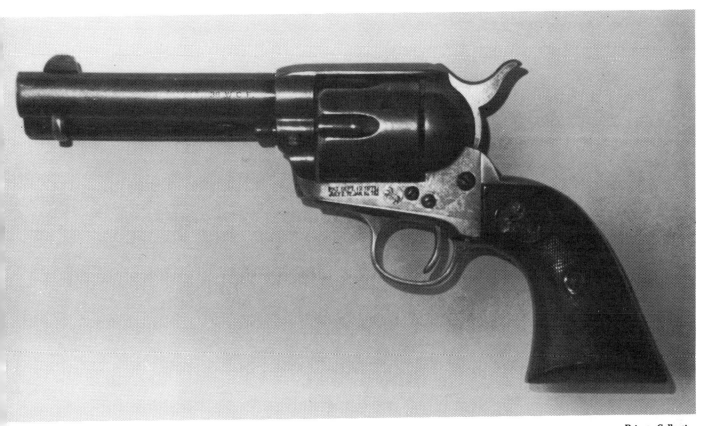

SN 198932. This .38-40 cal., 4 3/4" bbl., blue finish revolver was shipped August 28, 1900, to Krakauer, Zork & Moye Company, El Paso, Texas. Fourteen in shipment.

SN 65248. This .44-40 cal., 4 3/4" bbl., nickel finish revolver was manufactured in 1881 and sent back to Colt at a later date to be re-barrelled. This Colt was used by Cobb County, Georgia, Sheriff Bill Hutson. Shown with Sheriff Hutson's six-point star badge.

SN 237110. This .32-20 cal., 5 1/2" bbl. blue finish revolver was used by C. G. Davis, City Marshal of Burlington, Texas from 1905 - 1920. No factory information is available. Shown with the gun is the holster Marshal Davis used. The pearl grips are replacements.

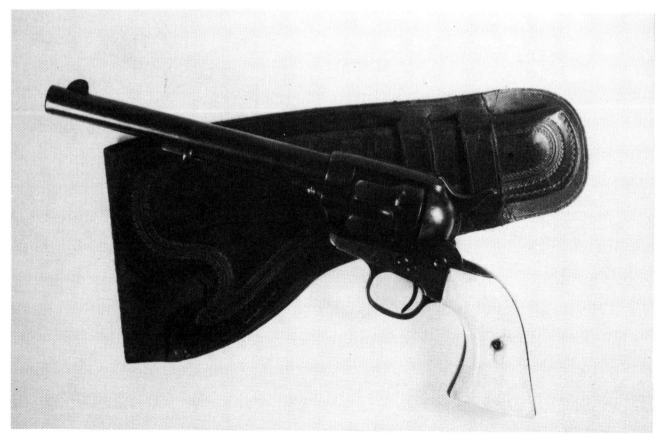

SN 145519. This .44-40, 7 1/2" bbl. blue finish was shipped on March 31, 1892 to Walter Tips, Austin Texas. Shipment of two. The ivory stocks are replacements.

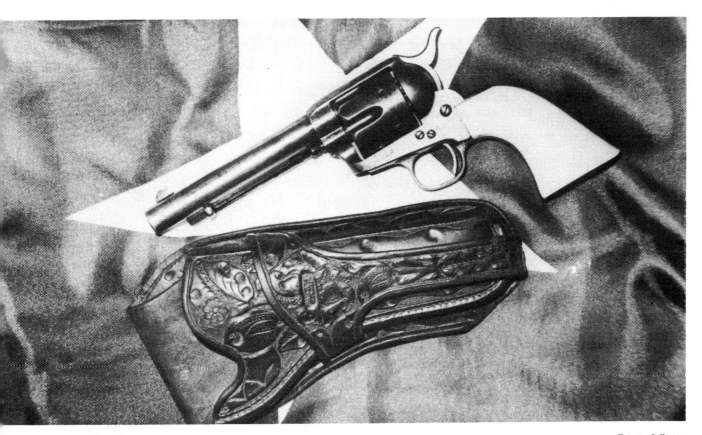

Private Collection

105075. This .45 cal., 5 1/2" bbl. revolver was manufactured in 1884. This revolver still has the original one-piece ivory ips. Shown with a nice Texas jock-strap holster marked S. D. Myres, El Paso, Texas.

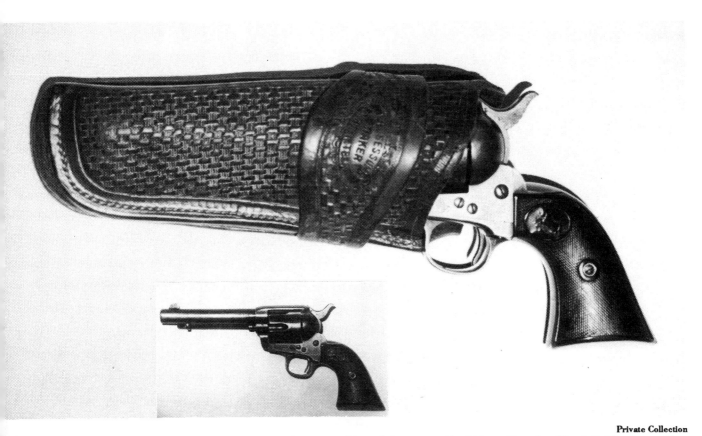

Private Collection

308060. This .41 cal., 5 1/2" bbl., blue finish revolver was shipped January 19, 1909, to Townley Metal & Hardware Co., ansas City, Missouri. Shown with lefthand single-loop basket weave holster marked, "L.A. Sessums, maker, Longview, Texas."

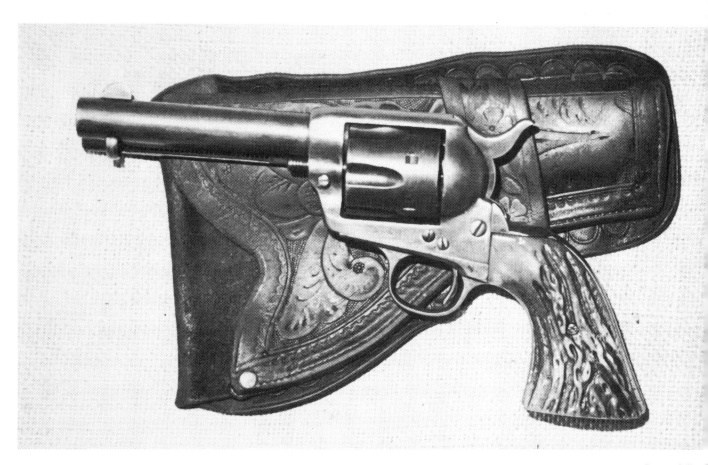
SN 249570. This .44-40 cal. Colt Frontier Six Shooter 4 3/4" bbl., blue finish revolver was shipped February 1, 1904 to Beri Cortes Hardware Co., Houston, Texas. Shipment of three. The stag grips are replacements. Shown with contemporary holst

SN 142356. This .41 cal., 4 3/4" bbl., blue finish revolver manufactured in 1891 was used by Lavaca County, Texas She Robert Wurm. Black powder .41 calibers are fairly scarce.

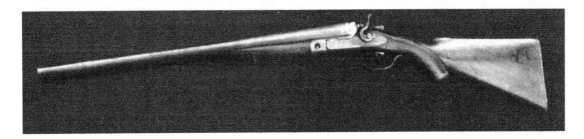

Parker Brothers 12 ga. hammer shotgun with 25&3/4" bbls. Serial #45197. Engraved on the rib is "Pinkerton Agency". To the right is shown the photo of the Pinkerton Man, Daniel McMurray and a special Pennsylvania Lines railroad pass issued to him.

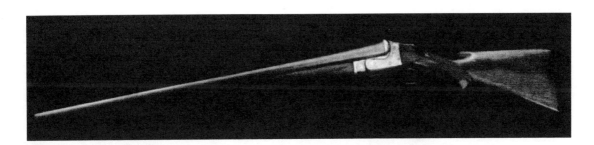

Ithaca 10 ga. double bbl. with 32" bbls. Serial #60852. Features an inscription on the top rib; "Presented to M.J. Larson by Wells Fargo & Co." To the left is a photo of the Wells Fargo Agent and his company identification card.

S.S.. Northcote 12 ga side lever hammer double bbl. shotgun with 20" bbls. Serial #11. Engraved on bbl. rib is;"Peter Pfiefer Bull's Head Saloon" and a picture of a bull's head. At left is his framed innkeeper's license, for 1885-86, his photo and a group of saloon girl photos. No doubt a useful weapon to keep order or discourage bad behavior of the patrons.

Colt New Service Revolver, 44-40 WCF caliber recovered from the body of one of Pancho Villa's bandits by a detachment of U.S. Cavalry, three of whom are shown at the right.
It is marked on the backstrap "Captured From Mexican Bandit During Pancho Villa Expedition".

This shotgun is a Janssen & Sons Co. 12 gauge double barrel, serial #9905. It is marked "Homestake" on the receiver and "HMC" on the barrel under rib.

This gun was the property of the Homestake Mining Company in the Dakota Territory.
A stock certificate from that company is shown at the left.

This shotgun was used by American Dredging Company to protect its Gold dredges working the rivers of the west.
It is a Union Arms Co., Toledo, Ohio 12 gauge double barreled shotgun with 20" barrels. Serial #5298.
It is marked on the buttstock "American Dredging Company".
A stock certificate from that company is shown above the gun.

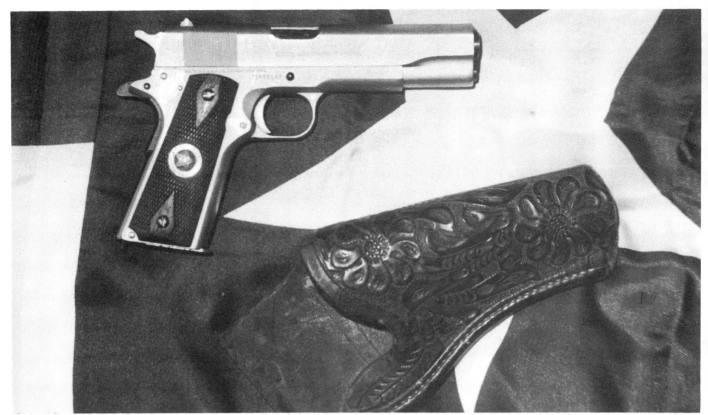

Private Collection

SN 70B50157. This Colt Mark IV Government Model, .45 cal. automatic was used by Texas Ranger Captain E.G. Albers, Jr., Company F, Waco, Texas. The backstrap is engraved "E.G. Albers, Jr., Texas Rangers, Captain Company F." The left grip has a Texas flag and the right has a small Ranger badge. The gun has a satin finish. Shown with a Texas holster marked Chas. Bluemel, El Paso, Maker.

E. G. Albers, Jr. served as Captain of The Texas Rangers, Company F, Waco, Texas.

N TR-49. This beautifully engraved .45 cal., 7 1/2" bbl. is a grade 2, D engraved special presentation model of the Texas Ranger Series produced in 1969. It is silver finish with one-piece ivory grips with Texas Ranger badge on left side. The engraving was done by Frank Hendricks.

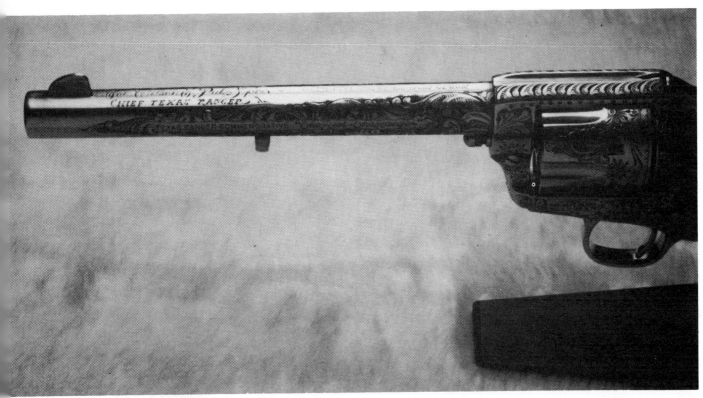

N TR-49. Left side view showing barrel engraving "Col. Wilson E. "Pat" Speir, Chief Texas Ranger". Colonel Speir served as Director of the Texas Department of Public Safety.

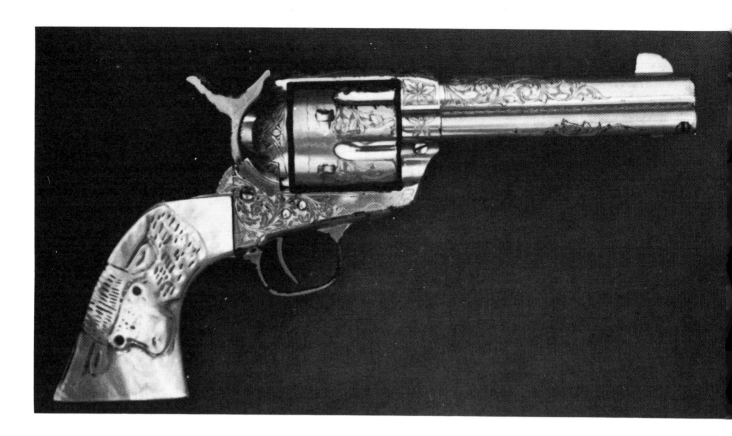

Collection of Morgan L. Mill[er]

SN 356841. This .45 cal., 4 3/4" bbl., nickel finish revolver with carved pearl ox head grips with ruby eyes was manufacture[d] in 1939. It has served two generations of Texas lawmen, Morgan Eugene & Morgan L. Miller

Morgan Eugene Miller was born on 04-29-06, in Dimmit County, Texas and he died of a heart attack on 11-29-59 in Tampico, Tamaulipas, Mexico. For many years until his death he was commissioned as a Special Ranger through the Texas Department of Public Safety and was employed as Special Agent for the Central Power and Light Company throughout south Texas. His job as Special Agent for CP&L involved conducting criminal and special investigations for CP&L and assisting other law enforcement agencies with their investigations. When he died he was conducting an investigation in Mexico for another law enforcement agency. His earlier law enforcement career included service as a Texas State Game Warden and Deputy Sheriff in several Texas counties.

MORGAN EUGENE MILLER

Collection of Morgan L. Miller

N 2753 SA. This early Post-War .38 Special Colt with 5 1/2" bbl. is owned and used by Texas Ranger Morgan L. Miller. The Colt .45 Automatic Government Model Serial No. 323611-C (inset) is the sidearm used daily by Texas Ranger Morgan L. Miller.

MORGAN L. MILLER

Morgan Louis Miller, son of Morgan Eugene Miller (opposite page), was born in Brownsville, Texas on 11-13-45. He is a Texas Ranger Sergeant presently stationed in Victoria, located on the Texas Gulf Coast, and is a member of Ranger Company "D" which encompasses forty counties of south Texas. He joined the Texas Department of Public Safety in 1968 and served as a Texas Highway Patrolman and Highway Patrol Sergeant prior to joining the Texas Rangers in 1978. He has been stationed in San Antonio, McAllen, and Kingsville with most of his service in Victoria. He also served fourteen months (1966-67) in Vietnam as a U.S. Army artillery sergeant.

Texas Ranger Special Edition

SN SA64343. This Colt .45 cal., 4 3/4" bbl., blue, SA revolver is one of 94 manufactured by Colt in early 1984 and sold directly to each Texas Ranger. "Texas Rangers" is etched in block style vertically down the backstrap. Number "22" is hand engraved in flush silver inlay at base of gun. Number 22 was Ranger James R. Peters' seniority number at that time.

Private Collection

44-40 W.C.F. caliber 4 & 3/4" barrel serial #193808. Engraved in the Helfricht style by Texas master engraver Dave Wade Harris. Features ivory grips with the Colt medallion.

Early 41 caliber Bisley model serial #195378. This revolver was shipped from the factory in 1900 to Zork Krakaur in El Paso, Texas. It features the original hard rubber grips.

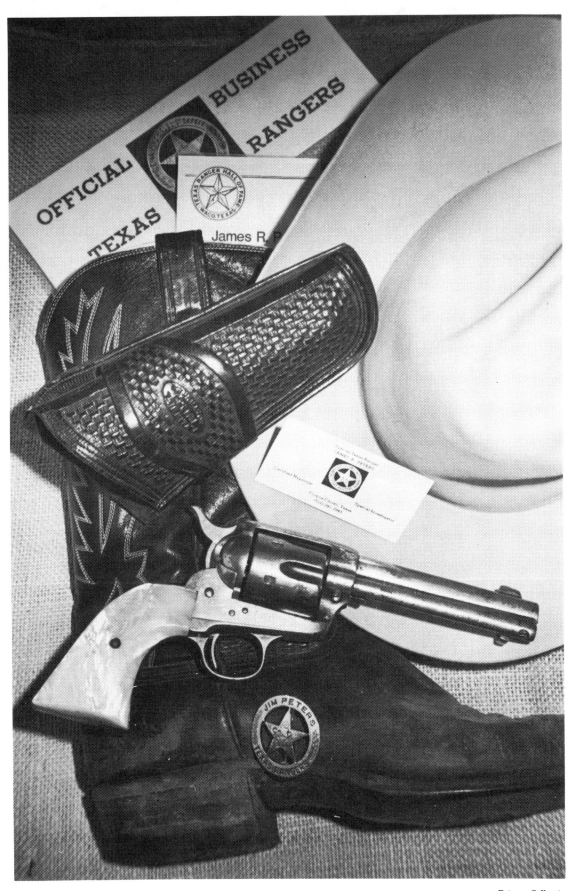

Private Collection

SN 193622. This .41 cal., 4 3/4" bbl., nickel finish with pearl grips was used by Texas Ranger James R. Peters. According to factory records the revolver was shipped March 1, 1900 to Walter Tips, Austin Texas. Shipment of two. All items shown were used by Ranger Peters. The holster is marked "A. W. Brill, Austin, Texas."

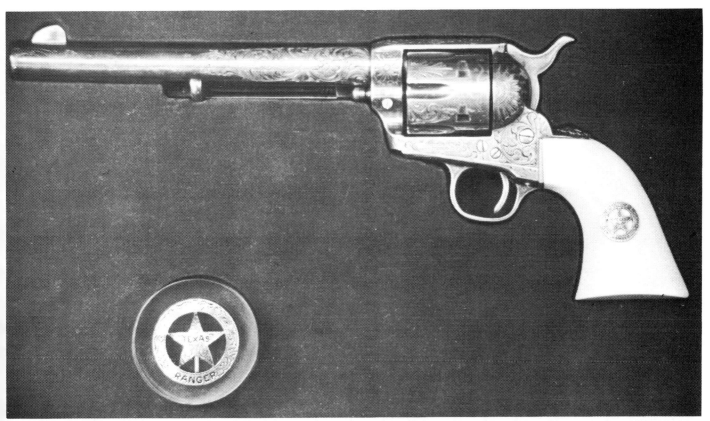

SN TR 156. One of 200 Presentation Models. This .45 cal., 7 1/2" bbl., Texas Ranger Commemorative was engraved and silver-plated by Frank Hendricks, San Antonio, Texas. Note miniature Texas Ranger badge in Ivory grip.

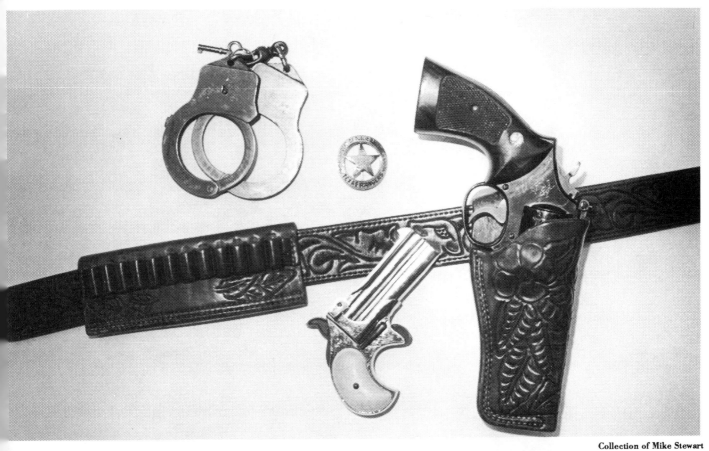

SN K899898 Smith & Wesson Model 19, 4" bbl., has Texas Public Safety markings and was issued to Ranger James R. Peters. Also shown are his belt & holster outfit, handcuffs, badge, and derringer used by Ranger Peters.

Colt Single action, 45 caliber, 5&1/2" bbl. ,serial # 2 of 250 Roy Rogers-Dale Evans Tribute Revolvers. One piece ivory grips with the Double R brand inlaid. Specially ordered by Roy Rogers Jr. and shipped directly to the museum.

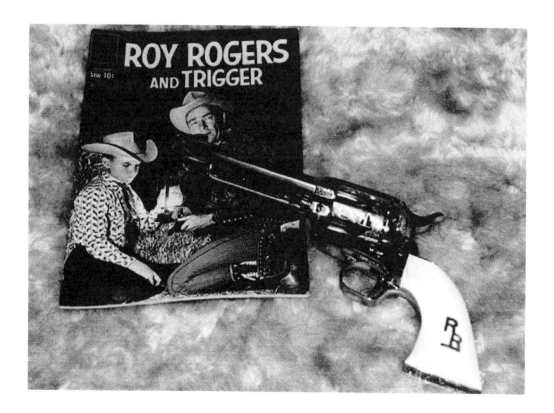

Colt Single Action, 45 caliber, 4&3/4" bbl., serial #PROTO-2, prototype for the Roy Rogers Premier, engraved and silver plated. Shipped to Roy at the museum.

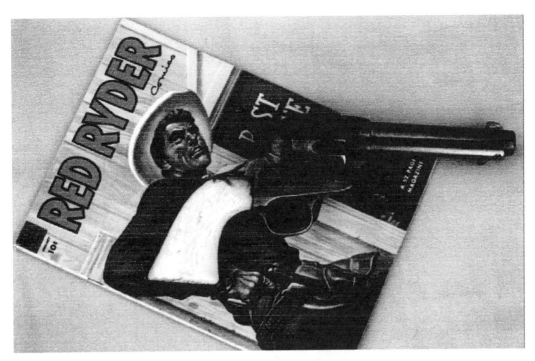

45 caliber 4&3/4" bbl., serial #65359, old one piece ivory grips, this Colt SAA was used by cowboy star Don "Red" Barry during his entire career including his first movie "Wyoming Outlaw". Barry was the first Red Ryder and a top Republic Studios cowboy star.

45 caliber, Colt SAA, serial #93955, engraved, with mother of pearl grips. It has been shot by Roy Rogers, Roy jr and Dustin Rogers. Presented to Roy in 1997, it was the last revolver Roy fired before his death on July 6, 1998.

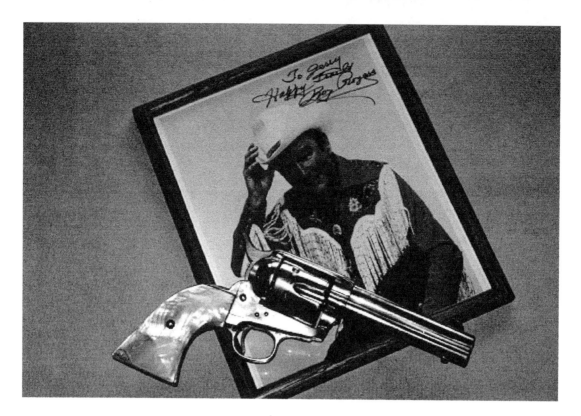

Colt SAA 44-40 caliber, 4&3/4", serial # 160062 bbl., nickel plated. From the Roy Rogers & Dale Evans museum. Last fired on December 20, 1997 by Roy Rogers jr. using antique shot shells bought from The Buffalo Bill Wild West Show by his father.

41 caliber, manufactured in 1898, serial #180601. Finish is an old renickeling with Hollywood style ivory grips. This Colt SAA, was owned by John Hart, "The Lone Ranger". John did 52 television episodes starring as the famous masked Ranger.

TEXAS RANGER BADGES FROM THE COLLECTION OF *Charles Schreiner, III and Paul Sorrell*

Circa 1909-1935 - Frank Hamer, Texas Ranger Captain

Circa 1930

Circa 1920-1935
Made by Simmang,
San Antonio, Texas

Texas Ranger Walter Russell's badge
Retired 1967

Johnny Krumnow
Houston, Texas, 1950 - 1960

Circa 1930

Capt. A. Y. Allee, Co. D
joined Rangers in 1931
Badge Circa 1935 - 68

Charles Ludlam, Texas Ranger, 1931

Circa 1928 - Dot E. Smith, Co. B, Texas Ranger, Deputy Sheriff, Lincoln County, Nevada, and Clark County, Nevada, Policeman, Las Vegas, Nevada. Marked Sterling

Circa 1926-1937
Captain J. W. McCormick, Texas Ranger.

First Department Public Safety issue in 1935 John R. Peavy, Texas Ranger, Deputy Sheriff, Chief Scout, U. S. Army and Border Patrol.

Circa 1940 - 1957

Circa 1920. Made by Los Angeles Rubber Stamp Co., Los Angeles, California.

Circa pre-1900

Special Texas Ranger, Jimmy Dee
Inspector, Texas & Southwestern
Cattle Raisers Association 1960-1970

Circa 1910 - 1920

Circa 1918-1925 - Texas Ranger Lee Tremble

Circa 1920

Probably one of the finest examples of a Texas Ranger badge known. Marked Texas Ranger, Co. D. Mfg. by L. F. Donnell Co., Chicago, Ill. Listed in Chicago City Directory 1880-1910. Cast in bronze and silver-plated.

White Porcelain with blue enamel letters. Back is bronze cast with blue. Presentation from Jo W. Allison. Manufactured by Charles M. Robbins Co., Attlebourghs, Mass.

Worn by "Lone Wolf" Gonzoles
Badge dated 6-10-27

Circa 1930 - 1940

Owned & Worn by Dott E. Smith
Police Chief, Camp Wolters, Texas
1940

Circa 1930

Circa 1900 - 1920

San Antonio, Texas Police Badge - Circa 1900

**San Antonio, Texas
Circa 1910**

Circa 1950

Circa 1950

**Worn by Porter Hart
Deputy Sheriff, Brazoria County, Texas
Circa 1930**

Circa 1890 - 1910

Circa 1920

Circa 1950

Texas Ranger A. Y. Allee's Badge
Circa 1930

Worn by Dott E. Smith
Circa 1939
Camp Wolters, Texas

Circa 1920

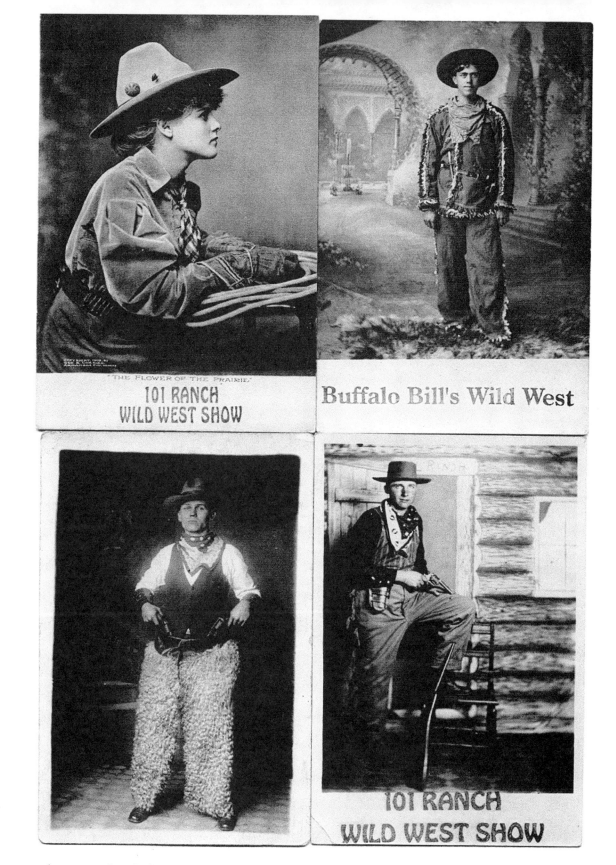

A group of real photograph postcards sold at the Wild West Shows or at the ranches where the "dudes" would go for vacations.

22 Long Rifle caliber Smith & Wesson target model. serial #126131. This 6" barrel revolver was acquired from the estate of the famous actor Clark Gable.

This Colt SAA, 45 caliber 4 & 3/4" barrel revolver, serial #177057 was used by Cy Compton, a performer in the famous Buffalo Bill's Wild West Show. The backstrap is marked " Buffalo Bill's Wild West Show" and the butt is marked "Cy Compton".

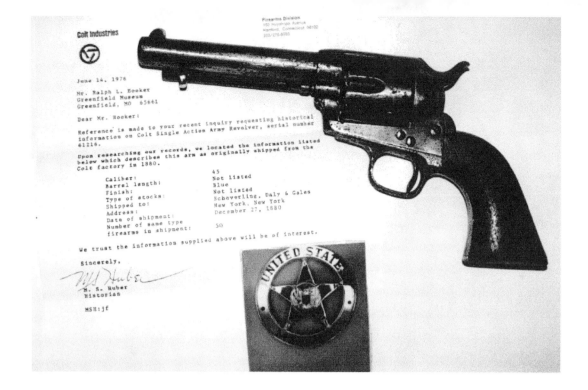

Colt SAA, 45 caliber, 5&1/2" bbl., serial #61216. This revolver was spaded up from a potato patch in Phelps, MO. and was purchased by the current owner for $5.00 ! It is shown with a Colt factory letter stating that it was shipped from the factory on December 27, 1880 to Schoverling, Daly & Gales in New York City.

32-20 caliber, 5&1/2" bbl. Colt Bisley from Ringling OK. It once belonged to Constable Joe Colson. The current owner, a U.S. Marshall, attributes the damaged grip to "a trouble I had with a young fellow."

Colt 32-20 caliber Bisley Model, 4&3/4" bbl., serial #319010. Formerly owned by famous silent movie Cowboy star Hoot Gibson.

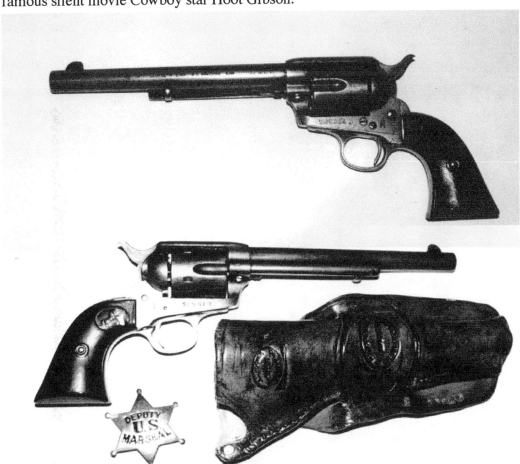

Colt SAA 38-40 caliber, 7&1/2" bbl., serial # 240040. Owned by Marshal Ralph L. Hooker. A famous photo shows this revolver being held by George Earp. Engraved on the barrel is " George W. Earp U.S. Marshall Kan." Holster is serial numbered to revolver.

Colt SAA 38-40 W.C.F. caliber, 4 & 3/4" barrel revolver, serial #209288 was manufactured in 1901. It was found buried in a ditch near Virgina City, Nevada. Here's a gun that could tell some stories!

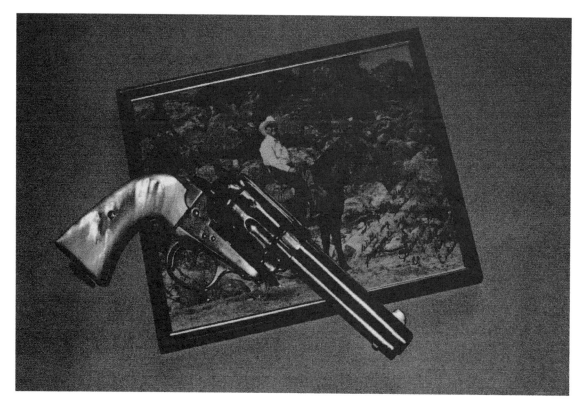

Colt SAA 45 caliber, 4 & 3/4" barrel serial #261935. Fitted with ivory grips and renickeled many years ago. This revolver was carried by George Frazier, a Texas Ranger with Co. E in San Angelo Texas.

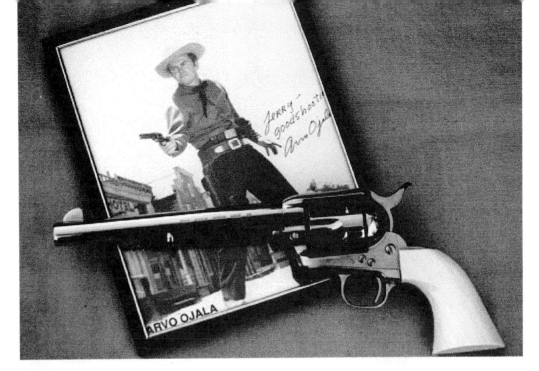

45 caliber 7&1/2 bbl., gold plated with one piece ivory grips. Serial #4. This third generation Colt letters directly to Arvo Ojala, the legendary Hollywood Shooting coach. This is the Gunsmoke Edition.

45 caliber 5&1/2" bbl. manufactured in 1873, serial #1646. This Colt is an early first year (Ainsworth Frame) Artillery Model. It was owned by cowboy star Rex Allen. Refinished many years ago, it has cowboy grips. Allen was known as "The Arizona Cowboy" and was one of the last silver screen cowboys.

38 Special, Bisley Model 5&1/2" bbl.., serial #263602 old reblue with old Hollywood stag grips, has movie markings (Stembridge Rental) on frame and "Tex Terry" on the butt. Terry was a "badman" in over 500 films, working with all the top stars including Roy Rogers and Gene Autry.

45 caliber, 7&1/2" bbl., serial #308422 with old renickel finish. This colt was owned and used by Big Buck Maffei, a 7"2" giant who acted in many westerns including Bonanza and the Alaskans. His name appears on the revolvers backstrap and holster rig (not shown).

Colt SAA 45 caliber 5 & 1/2" barrel, serial #8360SA manufactured in 1956, the first postwar year. This revolver is from the Hank Williams Jr. collection.

22 Long Rifle caliber Buntline Scout, serial #55235F. This early model is from the estate sale of Sammy Davis Jr. His name is engraved on the backstrap.

Colt SAA 45 caliber, 4&3/4" bbl., serial #348550. Shipped to Shelton-Payne Arms in El Paso Texas on March 12, 1926. This gun has been restored by Tommy Haas.

Colt SAA 38 Special 4&3/4" bbl, serial #301781. Given by Elmer Keith to Texas Lawman Bill Jordan. Fitted with 1860 Army backstrap and grips.

A collection of Wild West Show postcards featuring actual photographs as well as artistic interpretations of what cowboys and cowgirls might look like.

An unusual pair of souvenir bookends from the 101 Ranch Wild West Show. They are marked "101 Ranch Wild West Show" on each one.

A cowboy's tin coffee cup from the 101 Ranch or Wild West Show. It is marked "101" inside a banner on the front of the cup.

John Hart   *The Lone Ranger and Silver*

A few of the Colt Single Actions owned and used by John Hart, " The Lone Ranger". From left to right; 45 Long Colt and 45 ACP, 5&1/2" bbl., serial #2385SA, 44-40, 4&3/4" bbl., serial #25372A, two piece ivory grips, factory engraved on the backstrap "Presented To My Good Friend Mick LaFever from John Hart "The Lone Ranger", 357 Magnum 5&1/2" bbl. serial #53628SA, 45 Long Colt , Artillery Model, 5&1/2" bbl., serial #17101, 45 Long Colt, 4&3/4" bbl. serial #32395SA, full coverage engraving by Master Engraver Ben Shostle, two piece steer head carved ivory grips.

Two modern lever action rifles owned by John Hart. At top is a Browning BLR in 308 Winchester, serial #16K69. At bottom is a Winchester 94 Big Bore in 375 Winchester, serial #BB037904

John Hart did not limit himself to traditional western revolvers, although they are his favorites. Pictured here are some of his personal handguns. From the left; Smith & Wesson mdl 17 in 22 LR, serial #16K6409, Colt SAA 45 LC, 7&1/2" bbl, Hollywood stag grips and Serial numbers EEE121620 on the frame and 32851 on the trigger guard and butt, Colt Government Model 70 series in 45 ACP, serial #70B06296, Great Western SAA, 45 LC, 7&1/2" bbl. serial#17352, Ruger Vaquero, 45 LC, 4&3/4" bbl., serial #55-01494, Ruger Vaquero, 44-40, 4&3/4" bbl., serial #56-11810.

One of John Hart's (The Lone Ranger) favorite rifles is this very early Marlin Model 39, serial #279. It was purchased in 1938 and has been a fine shooter since then.

John states that it is the finest snap shooting rifle he has ever owned. It's never seen anything but Long Rifle ammunition which helps explain why it's still a very accurate rifle even after over 60 years of regular use.

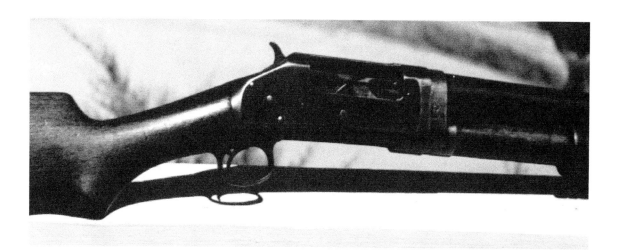

John acquired this Model 97 Winchester pump shotgun, serial #E844671, in 1957 from a Toronto, Canada gun shop where it had been a rental gun. (Imagine that in Canada today!)

He calls it a "Great Old Gun" and says he prefers it to more modern shotguns because it has an exposed hammer as did the revolvers and rifles he used in his movie and television career.

The 97 Winchester has appeared in many Western movies. It is perhaps most remembered for its use in "The Wild Bunch" where it's ability to fire seven shots quickly was used to good effect on the bad bandito soldiers.

The Winchester Model 52 has long been considered the finest American made 22 rimfire target rifle available. John Hart owns this early model, serial #29931, with the tangent rear sight and bbl. band. It is also equipped with blocks for target type telescopic sights. John says "It's really a treat to shoot."

This is a very early Winchester 22 caliber single shot Model 04. Let John tell the story of this little rifle; "My Uncle, after making sure that I kept it pointed straight up or straight down or only what I wished to shoot at, gave me the gun. I was 10 years old, boy oh boy, instant Daniel Boone. This little rifle is a gem with its fancy curved trigger guard. I only shoot it with 22 shorts out of respect for its age and they are more fun anyway."

Another of John Hart's favorite rifles is this custom 243 Winchester made for him by Weatherby. It is built on an FN Mauser action with a Douglas barrel. Sighting is provided by a 3-9 X Universal scope in Buehler mounts. A beautiful custom rifle perfectly suited to prairie dogs and deer in the desert country of California.